# The Social Problems of Children
# in Sub-Saharan Africa

# The Social Problems of Children in Sub-Saharan Africa

By

## Jerry W. Hollingsworth

CAMBRIDGE
SCHOLARS
PUBLISHING

The Social Problems of Children in Sub-Saharan Africa,
by Jerry W. Hollingsworth

This book first published 2012

Cambridge Scholars Publishing

12 Back Chapman Street, Newcastle upon Tyne, NE6 2XX, UK

British Library Cataloguing in Publication Data
A catalogue record for this book is available from the British Library

ISBN (10): 1-4438-4021-1, ISBN (13): 978-1-4438-4021-7

This book is dedicated to Dr. Robert Wallace,
long time teacher, amazing scholar, mentor, colleague,
and even more amazing friend.

# TABLE OF CONTENTS

# ACKNOWLEDGEMENTS

I have many early memories to lean on in the development of some of my ideas and visions. From an early age, I listened to my father tell stories about his adventures in Japan during the United States occupation after World War II. Those stories filled my head about world travel and cultures that were different from my own. Unfortunately, he passed before he realized that he had impacted me in such a way.

As an undergraduate Anthropology student, I would begin studying about different cultures, and that would become a permanent part of my intellectual journey. I would like to thank Dr. Gordon Bronitski for his impact on my early training in Anthropology. I would later transfer to McMurry University, where Dr. Robert Wallace convinced me that Sociology was a journey that would take me wherever I wanted to go. He was right. Without the guidance and mentoring from Robert Wallace, this project, along with any others would not have happened. His impact on my future has been undeniable, both while I was an undergraduate, and now as a colleague. He was also highly involved in the eventual shape this book would take. He has always kept me grounded academically, and for that, I owe a huge debt of gratitude.

I would also like to thank the United Methodist Church Higher Education Authority, who contributed funding for this study in Africa by awarding me the Sam Taylor Fellowship. I am deeply grateful to their commitment to higher education, and academic research. I would also like to thank the Mercy Orphanage in Accra, Ghana, for allowing me to complete an in-depth investigation into the developmental functioning of orphans. Many thanks also to the International Field Research Expedition organization for placing me in some strategic positions in West Africa, where I was able to collect the needed data for this book.

A number of other individuals also deserve my thanks. Hugh Wiegel, from Towson University, was my companion in Africa who traveled with me and offered his friendship during my stay there. I was later honored to serve on his thesis committee. He is on the way to becoming an influential scholar on African studies. Thanks to Adam De Sousa, from Canada, as well as Haseeb Fatma, who trekked out to the Millennium Village in Bonsaaso in the rural villages with me. It was a long and tiring journey. I would also like to thank a number of individuals who befriended me while in Africa: Nina Rise, Tarrah Waters, Meghan Waters, Katy Rice, (my running companion while there), LRae Unruh, and Crystal Allison. Your friendship during this time meant a great deal to me.

I would also like to thank Mr. Anas Aremeyaw Anas, from Accra, an investigative journalist who gave me permission to include the information from his report on the abuse at the Osu Children's Home. Ana has been a champion for the rights of children in Africa, and has received a medal from President Obama for his recent work in uncovering a child trafficking ring in Ghana.

My thanks also must include Dr. Paul Fabrizio, Vice-President for Academic Affairs at McMurry University, who has continued to encourage me through my journeys to the developing world, on what he dubs my "poverty tour." Many thanks also to Dr. John Russell, President of McMurry University, who always has an encouraging word about my work. Thanks to all who have supported me in my endeavors, including Dr. Mark Waters, and Tim Kennedy. Special thanks to my lovely wife, Beth, who is always there when I return.

To all my friends in Ghana, I say, Okokroko Nyame, Obaatan pa Nyame Omfa ne Sunsum mmo mo ho ban. Ye da moa se. May the great God surround the people, living and dead, with his great love and protection.

—Jerry W. Hollingsworth

# INTRODUCTION

There is something magical about traveling the world. Of course, as a tourist, you enter a country with great expectations. Perhaps you have looked at guidebooks and identified several key areas you would like to visit. You pick out a nice hotel, or you examine restaurants, transportation possibilities, and a host of other amenities that will make your visit more appealing. That's traveling like a tourist. That's fun, and there's nothing wrong with that. Traveling to third world countries examining social problems of children and conducting qualitative field work, however, is quite another story.

Instead of checking into a nice hotel with plenty of conveniences, you check into a hostel or other type of "group facility" where other workers are also staying. You might take a job as a volunteer, or a caseworker, or some other temporary position. You work yourself into an environment where you can see the problems firsthand, either in a hospital, an orphanage, school, or similar facility. In some ways, it is incredible to work in these types of organizations. More often than not, you meet terrific people who are out to make a difference in the world. I have worked alongside medical students, lawyers, doctors, social workers, teachers, students, and volunteers from all over the world. As a result, I have friends in different countries I still keep in touch with.

An Ethnographer also directly encounters the population they are observing. They may or may not let others know that they are on a research project. They are in a unique position to observe firsthand, the culture, the behaviors, lifestyles, and activities of the group in which they are interested in studying. If anyone knew that they were being studied, there is the distinct possibility that some behaviors may change, for several reasons. Some may want to appear more socially acceptable, thus giving you a false impression.

In other circumstances, I have told most of my subjects that they were part of a study, and eventually, they just accepted me and forgot all about the research. It is up to the Ethnographer whether or not they should inform the subjects, but good ethics might require that a standard permission be granted, as well as a brief overview of the research that is taking place. Interviews actually become easier, because you are there. It is also quite humbling for a professor who is used to standing in front of a classroom, to be working with orphans, holding them in your lap as they urinate down your leg, or following a street child to his cardboard box house to see where they live. It brings the developing world to an "up close and personal" view.

The downside is that you may be alone in a foreign country, and vulnerable to certain conditions, such as robbery or kidnapping. Foreigners from Western countries are mostly considered "rich" by those in poor countries, and at times, can be targets of muggings and street crimes. Situating yourself in a high crime area in slums, shanty towns, or out in the streets observing conditions, you may inadvertently be putting yourself in harm's way, and increase your chances of becoming a victim. Since 9-11, Americans are vulnerable in certain locales, and may be potential kidnapping victims.

Other downsides to working in these types of environments are possible medical problems. Some hospitals are poorly operated, with less than adequate resources, such as physicians, nurses, or other major medical personnel. Sometimes, blood supplies are even contaminated, and if you are in need of a blood transfusion, that could create numerous difficulties. My physician has constantly nagged me to take my own blood on my journeys to such places at Sub-Saharan Africa because of these conditions, but I could never bring myself to try that.

An Ethnographer working in these conditions in developing countries may also have to prepare for such things as malaria. One of the major drugs available for preventing malaria is Lariam, which I took before I left, during my stay there, and then for another month after returning home. The medicine works great preventing malaria, but has some nasty side effects. It may cause nightmares that can be extreme or may cause depression that can become debilitating to some people. I've seen many grown men crying in the night for no reason that they can think of. I have heard people screaming in the night from horrible dreams that were haunting them. Being away from home and family may intensify the depression and anxiety, as well.

In some regard, this style of research follows the style of Erving Goffman, who would immerse himself into his chosen area of interest. For example, Goffman posed as a pseudo-employee of St. Elizabeth's Hospital for a year, and collected ethnographic data on selected aspects of patients' social life (Goffman, 1961). Other noted sociologists have used this method to study such topics as drug use, crime, and homelessness. For this study, I set out to examine the life of children who live in orphanages in Sub-Saharan Africa. Several questions instantly arose as I mapped out my plan of study. For example, how and why do children end up in an orphanage in the first place? What are the orphanages like in Africa? How does it affect development of children who are living there, both socially and cognitively? What are the long-term implications of being an orphan?

While the original intention of this work was to study orphans and orphanages, the situation quickly developed into a much deeper subject. Out of necessity, I was charged with looking at other social problems that were present in Sub-Saharan Africa. Orphans, I found out were vulnerable populations, and were perfect targets for child molesters, military recruiters, traffickers, employers looking for cheap labor, and other reprehensible situations. Thus, I felt it was important to include other social problems of children into the study.

## From Latin America to Africa

This study actually follows my original study on the street children of Latin America in my first book, *Children of the Sun: An Ethnographic Study of the Street Children of Latin America.* While studying street children there, I was appalled at the living conditions of people and children that were living in slums and shanty towns in Mexico and Peru. The nature of that work influenced me to project myself into the Continent of Africa, where I traveled to Ghana, in West Africa to continue observing the conditions of children there. However, when I landed in Africa, I was amazed at the number of people living in those conditions. In Latin America, there seemed to be pockets of prosperity, but in Africa, those pockets of prosperity were few and far between. As a matter of fact, the more I observed in Africa, the more problems I discovered.

Family life of society is also put under the microscope in the culture of Sub-Saharan Africa, and as a result, a number of questions begged to be answered. For example, what do we expect from the family unit? How does the family unit in Sub-Saharan Africa differ from family life in the United States? What other social problems do children in Sub-Saharan Africa suffer from?

## Expectations for Children in Western Society

Western societies, especially U.S. society have a somewhat contradictory idea of what childhood should be. On one hand, we feel like children should play, surrounded by this idea of innocence and play. Some of our fondest memories as adults are of the times when we were children and had no cares that adults faced. Yet, in between those years, adults have insisted on moments when children should be studying, working, improving, and stimulating their brains. Therefore, we encourage educational activities and create an environment where essential development takes place.

However, in some cultures, this is not possible, as children are abandoned to live on their own as orphans, street children, or become exploited in many other ways. In Latin America, street children have become "pseudo-adults" at very early ages (Hollingsworth, 2008). In other cultures, such as Sub-Saharan Africa, although families are important, it is not always possible to maintain those family connections with children, especially when the adult population is dying off due to HIV/AIDS.

## Setting and Methodology

For the purposes of this study, I lived in a tiny fishing village in Ghana, West Africa, known as Teshie. I worked in several orphanages in Ghana, to get a real picture of what life was like inside an African orphanage. I also interviewed other workers in other orphanages to get an idea of what they were like. I walked the streets in Accra, the capital city, as well as Kumasi, the second largest city in Ghana to observe street children, as well. I observed Cape Coast, and the Slave Castles, where the Colonial powers such as Portugal, Spain, The Dutch, and the British held slaves in dungeons during the Atlantic Slave Trade era. I observed and conducted interviews in as many areas as possible to get a real picture of these social problems in an ethnographical sense.

## What Are Social Problems?

According to sociologists, a social problem exists when an influential group asserts that a certain social condition affecting a large number of people is a problem that may be remedied by collective action (Zastrow, 2000). For instance, they refer to the influential group as one that appears capable of having a significant impact on social policy at the national level. For the purposes of this book, the United Nations may be just such an influential group on an international level, along with several other International organizations, policy makers, and Institutions, such as UNICEF, the World Bank, and the International Monetary Fund. These organizations have been leading the way into discovering and addressing the problems of children in developing countries, and especially on the Continent of Africa. In this volume, we will also investigate these organizations, as well as their policies, and their activities concerning the social problems of children in Sub-Saharan Africa.

Social problems must also affect a large population of people. If they affect only isolated individuals, they may be personal problems but not social problems. Accordingly, the Sociologist C. Wright Mills explains this concept as understanding the *Sociological Imagination*, (1959), or the ability to see the relationship between individual experiences and the larger society. Social problems are social because they are so widespread that they affect society itself.

This study should demonstrate that large enough numbers of children are affected by child soldiering, child labor, sexual exploitation, street children, and orphans in the developing world and thus are fully deserving of the title: social problems.

## The Problem

Currently, UNICEF estimates the number of Street Children around the world at 150 million. Those numbers are more than the combined populations of either Russia or Japan. Orphans are estimated at another 140 million. The International Labor

Organization (ILO), a UN agency, estimates the number of child laborers at 250 million. There are another 1.5 million children being trafficked each year for labor or sexual purposes.

If these numbers are not substantial enough to call these issues a social problem, then nothing is. Therefore, I will be presenting my picture of these child difficulties as social problems in the strict sociological sense, and presenting my case through statistics by influential groups such as UNICEF, The United Nations, The International Labor Organization, as well as International reports such as the Children on the Brink series, which gathers data on such topics as AIDS Orphans in Africa.

Another contributing factor in examining issues as social problems is that these social conditions may be remedied by collective action. Collective action can be described as strikes, demonstrations, public service advertising, lobbying, and formation of interest groups. In the area of social problems with children in a global setting, it has long been thought that these were conditions that were unchangeable. That sort of thinking must be abandoned in favor of collective action in the form of governmental groups, national agencies, the United Nations, Micro lending institutions, and Non-Governmental Agencies around the world to bring about lasting change for some of these problems.

## Background and Experience

I suppose I have a unique background for the work I am presenting here. Most of my academic credentials are specialized in several fields. Although I am sociologically trained, I have a Social Work background, and that is where I spent thirteen years in the field, working with children. My Doctoral work was also very specific, in that it trained me for my further work in children's problems. I am also anthropologically inclined, which means that I have a keen desire to get out into the field and observe social conditions firsthand, ethnographically.

My first book, *Children of the Sun: an Ethnographic Study of the Street Children of Latin America,* was an exploration into the culture of Street Children in Mexico and Peru. Delving into those problems directly led to the development of this study, which takes into account problems of children in Sub-Saharan Africa.

The statistics and the indexes, and the coefficients, and the reports from International research all make sense to me, but I find it particularly fascinating to try to live in those conditions as much as possible to get a feel of what poverty is like from an observation viewpoint. This is qualitative analysis in a nut shell. My academic training leads me to believe that one gain a greater understanding of a problem when they enter the field and observe, interview, or otherwise live with the people who are experiencing social problems.

While this is a great tool, sometimes it has its drawbacks. For example, when I first returned to the United States from Africa, I had a terrible time adjusting. I went to lunch at one of my favorite Chinese buffet restaurants, and after a few moments of watching people pile food high on their plates, and then returning to the buffet line for seconds and thirds, I had to leave. I was no longer the same person I was before I went to West Africa. I still had visions in my head of children living in an orphanage, eating one or two bowls of rice a day and crying themselves to sleep at night because they were hungry. I could remember the children in Mexico and Peru that huffed glue and other dangerous substances so they could numb the hunger pangs.

On the other hand, I have to admit, that at times, even I am often desensitized to the information I am working with. Recently, I was invited as a guest speaker at the University of Arkansas for their annual Sociology Alpha Kappa Delta event. The room was full to capacity as I began my presentation. I was presenting data that pertained to a good portion of what is contained in this book: orphans in developing countries, child trafficking, etc...and I proceeded with great gusto, trying to communicate well, and with complete emphasis on my performance. After all, I was on stage in front of hundreds of people. When I was done, and it was time for questions, I looked up as they turned the lights up and I noticed that people were sporadically sniffing and crying. It dawned on me afterward that not everyone was used to seeing the facts, figures, and worst of all, the pictures that represent the many social problems of children in developing countries.

While it is not my intention to unfairly trigger emotional responses for the reader, I will present the information as clearly and accurately as possible. The information contained herein is often unpleasant and sometimes surprising. It's sometimes difficult to believe that some parts of the world can be so bad. It is hard to witness children starving, or living in squalor, when, in the developed world, we have so much, especially in the light of the "promise of globalization."

# CHAPTER ONE

# CULTURE, HISTORY, AND FAMILY LIFE

## Arrival in Ghana

As my plane landed at the Kotoka International Airport in Accra, I was greeted with one of the many con games practiced by airport security. It was a well-practiced routine; one improved over time on their part, and one that depends on the naiveté of the innocent traveler.

First, they asked you if you have made contact with the parties that will be picking you up at the airport. If you say no, they will offer to contact them for you, using their cell phone. Afterwards, they aggressively suggest that you owe them for the service they provided. It's a "shakedown," and a very efficient one, especially since they are wearing a uniform. It's also not a good first impression of Ghana, but was also indicative of the massive poverty that existed there.

I was waiting for my official greeting party from the organization I was working for. It was a non-profit Non-governmental Organization known as the IFRE (the International Field Research Expedition). After finally meeting my group, I felt more secure, as I fended off at least a half-dozen more of Airport Security on my own before having to give up a few more dollars. I soon was joined by several others who would also be taking positions in various places in orphanages or hospitals, or schools in the greater Accra region of Ghana. The IFRE is a placement agency who is in contact with the many orphanages in Africa and provides qualified volunteers for a fee.

Most of the volunteers I met would be working inside the various agencies in Ghana, and would be staying in the same central location, and would report daily to their assigned positions. We would sleep at the central compound, take all our meals there, and basically reside there during the time of our employment at our various jobs. It was more like a glorified dormitory.

The agency would also contribute to our field of knowledge in other ways, such as giving us a basis of understanding the language there. We would receive classes on the culture of Ghana, as well as lessons in Twi, one of the 57 different dialects of the Akkan language of Ghana. Twi is spoken by about 50 percent of the people in Ghana. The organization would also provide us with trips to different areas of the country to help us understand the culture and the country better, which I thought would be very important in working with the children in the orphanages. In my work with street children in Peru and Mexico, I ended up spending a couple of years studying Spanish and the culture in order to understand the children's basic culture. I would not have enough time to totally grip the languages in Ghana, but fortunately, most people would be able to understand English, as English was the official language of Ghana, due to British Colonialism.

As we made our way through the streets of Accra from the airport area to our compound, it was an eye-opening experience. All around me, citizens carried large bundles of objects on their heads, carrying them with ease. As we approached our destination, the streets became less passable, and the paved roads disappeared. Houses and neighborhoods became more rundown. Naked children ran down the dirt roads, along with a large numbers of dogs, goats, and chickens.

As one government official told me later, you could see what areas the British had occupied, as the roads were well-paved, but once you got outside of that central district, the roads were particularly bad. I noticed that right away as we bounced along the dirt roads in the area known as Teshie.

Teshie was a small fishing village just outside the Greater Accra area. It was about one step up from a shanty town. The people here lived in small shacks, with no running water, no electricity, and no conveniences. The people were largely fishermen, craftspeople, or small store-owners. Large numbers of the people there were also poor and unemployed. The majority of the people grew small amounts of vegetables around their homes, and owned a few goats or chickens. Most of the people living in the village spoke either Twi, or Ga, another one of the local dialects.

As we made our way to the compound where we would be staying, we made our way across the ruts and the holes in the dirt roads. Nothing was paved. Transportation in the area consisted of beat-up and aging minivans the locals called "Tro-Tro's." These vehicles ran periodically through the dirt roads providing a way for citizens to get into the greater Accra region. They ran even when the ruts in the roads were so deep that it doubled the amount of time it took to get to the city. During the monsoon season, the rains would come and damage the roads even more, deepening, and widening the ruts as more and more Tro-Tro's ran through the roads.

Amazingly, we bounced our way to our new home, the compound where I would be living the rest of the summer.

The compound was a multi-room dwelling, much like a college dormitory, if you discounted the mosquito nets hanging from the bunks, and the fact that there were no restroom facilities in the building, and no running water. What was in place for using the restroom in the compound were two outside toilets, which were equipped with commodes, but no running water. Collected rain water was used to pour down the toilets to essentially flush them into one of the many open sewers that existed outside the compound. Two 30-gallon barrels would be refilled each night as the rains tumbled off the building. If it did not rain, we cut back on our "flushing" until the rains came again, filling the barrels.

Fresh water was delivered to the compound by truck once a week and the water could be used for showering, but not drinking. We were limited to using one five-gallon bucket of this water for showering per day. Taking a shower consisted of filling up a plastic bucket and taking it into an enclosed area and pouring the water over your head. It was primitive, but after a few days, it was much in demand. I quickly began to look forward to my daily shower, as the temperatures were constantly in the 80's (F) with humidity ranging between 85-100%.

For drinking water, the facility provided us with treated water in small plastic bags which was safe to drink. We simply tore off one corner of the bag and drank the water out of the bag. We took our meals outside under a canopy. The meals were typically West African, and usually consisted of such local favorites as fried yams (which tasted almost identical to fried potatoes), or Foo-Foo, a local favorite consisting of a starchy mass of Cassava, mixed with Plantains. It was eaten by dipping your fingers into a rich, spicy soup and swallowing it without chewing. The cooks would work on the Foo-Foo for hours, pounding the Cassava in a large wooden bowl with wooden sticks, a custom that obviously went back centuries and was still in use.

We ate other typical West African foods, called Kenkey, which consisted of a boiled corn meal ball, wrapped in corn husks. It is eaten in a similar manner as the Foo-Foo, by pinching off a piece of the corn meal ball and dipping it into a spicy fish soup. We were also provided with a quantity of rice and a Cassava dish that was served with a spicy sauce.

The volunteers that were staying in the compound were from all over the world. There were medical students, social workers, college students, retired professors and others who were volunteering in a variety of ways. My job was working inside one of the NGO (Non-governmental Organization) orphanages, or a private concern that operated in the local area of Teshie. Others were working in a very large State-run facility in Osu, a neighborhood inside Accra, the capital city.

I was also afforded the opportunity to compare orphanages from two much different perspectives. While primarily working inside a private orphanage, I was able to observe the State facility as well, and was able to interview the workers and volunteers that were involved in the daily activities there. It was interesting to observe how different the two facilities were in the ways they were operated, how they were staffed, and the differences they offered in quality care. I would also get to travel to different locations to examine orphanages throughout the country. What I found was a variety of different operations, both good and bad. The observations inside these orphanages, and the interviews with street children led me into different areas that will be addressed in later chapters.

## The Republic of Ghana

The Republic of Ghana (formerly known as the Gold Coast) lies on the Gulf of Guinea on the Western coast of tropical Africa. It is bordered to the west by Cote d'Ivoire (the Ivory Coast), to the north by Burkina Faso, to the west by Togo and to the south by the Atlantic Ocean. It is a country with a total land mass area of about the size of the state of Oregon. It is not a huge country, occupying 30th place between Guinea and Uganda among the 47 countries of mainland Africa (Briggs, 2004).

The capital of Ghana is Accra, situated on the Atlantic coast, and has a population of about three million people. The second largest city in Ghana is Kumasi, the former capital of the Ashanti Tribal Empire, with a population of about one million. The total population of Ghana is approximately 20 million, with a population density of 80.0 persons per square kilometer.

Once a former British colony, Ghana was the first African country to be granted independence, and Kwame Nkrumah became the first president. Most of the country speaks some English, but at least four ethno-linguistic groupings exist in abundance there, including Fante, Akan, Ashante, Ewe, Mole-Dagbani, and Ga. However, there are at least 75 different African languages and many other dialects spoken in Ghana.

The geography of Ghana is an interesting diversity of low-lying flat areas of below 150 kilometers, to the Atlantic coastline, and then flanked by mountains to the east and west. The eastern highlands, part of the Togo-Atakora range that stretches all the way to the country of Benin, and reach altitudes of over 900 meters near the Togolese border. The highest mountain peak is Mount Afedjato. Most of southern Ghana is naturally covered in rainforest, while the central and northern parts of the country consist of savannahs, which are drier and more sparsely vegetated.

## Historical Background

The study of ancient history of Ghana recognizes that humans have been living in modern day Ghana for over 300,000 years, and others suggest that humans have lived there for millions of years (Briggs, 2004). The people that occupied ancient Ghana were hunters and gatherers, who lived in small clans of 25-50 people, living a nomadic existence. Some experts believe that the people became more pastoral and agriculturally inclined about 5000 BC. By 2000 BC, cattle and other animals were being domesticated, and several small villages had been established. Around 1000 AD, Ghana was becoming more urbanized, with several villages containing more than 2,000 people (Briggs, 2004).

Ancient Ghana was also the first source of West African gold to be exploited by the Trans-Saharan trade. One Iranian scholar who comprised material for an encyclopedia of the Muslim world wrote the following statement in the year 900:

It is said that beyond the source of the Nile is darkness and beyond the darkness are waters which make the gold grow…to the town of Ghana is a three-month's journey through deserts. In the country of Ghana gold grows in the sand as carrots do, and is plucked at sunrise.

Other stories abound, that tell of Ashanti Kings dressed in gold, and his entire court elaborately adorned with it (Reader, 1997). Prior to the arrival of the Portuguese in the late 15th century, merchant caravans would cross the Sahara desert from the North to the South, bringing such things as salt, fine cloth, and other luxury items which they would trade for goods like gold and ivory. These trade routes are thought to have existed as far back as 500 B.C. The area has always been a chief source of ivory, gold, and Kola nuts. These same products prompted the spread of Islam into West Africa, and later, led to the arrival of the Portuguese, who sought the same items (Reader, 1997).

In more recent history, Ghana was essentially at the epicenter of European maritime trade out of West Africa, while the Ashanti Empire gave political and social cohesion to much of the area. The modern state of Ghana did not officially take place until 1873, as it became a British holding, then known as the Gold Coast Colony.

# The Atlantic Slave Trade

Along the coast of Ghana, there are over sixty European forts and castles which are reminiscent of the long-standing and horrific Atlantic Slave Trade. This is indeed true of the entire Western coast of Africa, from where the Sahara desert ends in the north to the Cape of Good Hope in the south. Cape Coast Castle served as the British headquarters in Africa who was involved in the Atlantic Slave Trade, along with the Portuguese, the Spanish, the French, the Dutch, the Danes, and the Swedes. Most of these castles are still standing, and Cape Coast is now a UNESCO World Heritage site.

The Transatlantic Slave Trade was the greatest forced migration in history. From the mid-fifteenth to the late nineteenth century, over 11 million people born in Africa were carried across the ocean. About 3 million of those were taken by ships belonging to British merchants. Nearly a million enslaved Africans went to Jamaica alone. Life was extremely difficult on the slave ships, where captured Africans would be subject to fears of shipwreck, epidemics, and hungry sharks. Large numbers of sharks were known to follow slave ships for hundreds of miles, waiting for rebellious Africans to be thrown overboard, or waiting for those who were willing to swim to safety at any cost (Rediker, 2007).

In Ghana, in particular, Cape Coast was a major transition area for the Atlantic Slave Trade. Today, its walls still hold secrets long held of abuse, death, living in excrement in dark dungeons, followed by walking through what was known as the "Door of no return," as they were eventually loaded onto a slave ship bound for the Americas.

In examining the numbers of Africans sent as slaves from West Africa, it becomes an eye-opening experience. The sheer numbers reveal a booming enterprise for over 200 years. For example, between 1601 and 1650, over 503,000 Africans were kidnapped, imprisoned, and shipped through the famed "middle passage" to America. In the following years, between 1651 and 1700, another 750,000 Africans were shipped. Beginning in the seventeen hundreds, the numbers increased drastically. In the years 1701-1750, the numbers of Africans shipped increased to well over 2 million, and the fifty years that followed, almost 4 million were shipped. Most of these shipments were made by the Portuguese and the British. The Portuguese accounted for over 46 percent of those numbers, and the British made up 28 percent. The rest of the smaller percentages were performed by The French at 13 percent, followed by the Dutch with 5 percent and even the United States settled in at 5 percent.

Most of these Africans were shipped to Brazil and Jamaica. In fact, 41 percent of the total numbers of slaves were sent to Brazil, and 11 percent of the total went to Jamaica. Other destinations were the Spanish Caribbean, Barbados, English-speaking North America and other Caribbean locations.

## Effects on Ghana

According to scholars, the effects of the Atlantic Slave Trade on Ghana were devastating, draining their societies of the fittest, most capable young men and women in the population (St. Clair, 1999). Since more men were taken than women, the Atlantic Slave Trade in Ghana resulted in a gender imbalance by as much as 25 percent, and a total population decline of over 10 percent.

## Visiting Slave Castles

Walking through these slave castles is an experience one never forgets. They are hot, stifling, dark places, and the guide that took us through Cape Coast Castle put us in the dungeon and closed the door. Immediately, we fell into a darkness that was so complete that we were overwhelmed both mentally and physically. The atmosphere was ghostlike, and unnerving, knowing that people were held here against their will, with no alternatives. They would be chained together, naked, and forced to stand in their own excrement until ships showed up to transfer them to the Americas as slaves. In some of the dungeons, brown stains still exist waist high from the human excrement that captured Africans deposited there over the years.

## Modern Ghana

### Religion

Freedom of religion is a constitutional right in Ghana, and Islamic populations and Christians live side by side in relative tolerance. The largest group of religious believers in Ghana is Pentecostal, or Charismatic Christians, and they represent about 24 percent of the population. Protestants number about 18.6 percent, and Muslims represent about 15.6 percent. The rest of the numbers are made up of Catholics, and traditional tribal believers. Catholicism was introduced by the Portuguese in the late 15th Century. However, as the Portuguese departed Ghana in 1637, their influence waned.

# Standard of Living

## Poverty

Just to say that someone in some country is poor really doesn't mean anything. There are poor people everywhere, even in richer countries. Poverty can actually be measured, and the World Bank has defined an international standard for analyzing poverty around the world. The World Bank, established in 1944, is headquartered in Washington, D.C., with more than 10,000 employees in more than 100 offices worldwide. The World Bank is an international financial institution that provides loans to developing countries for capital programs. The World Bank's official goal is the reduction of poverty (World Bank, 2000).

Poverty is usually measured as either *extreme*, (absolute) or *moderate* (relative). Currently, the World Bank has set the international poverty standard as living on less than $1.25 a day for *extreme poverty and $2.00* per day for *moderate poverty*. It estimates that "in 2001, 1.1 billion people had consumption levels below $1 a day and 2.7 billion lived on less than $2 a day."

While in some quarters, Ghana is the shining light of Africa, it still has a long way to go, economically. Ghana has 30 percent of its population still living below the poverty line, which estimates their income at less than 1.25 US dollars per day. Education is also lacking there, with only about 45 percent of the children attending secondary schools.

Some other appalling facts about Ghana, is the lack of safe water and sanitation. Nineteen percent of households do not have access to toilet facilities, according to the Ghana Living Standard Survey taken in 2007. Only ten percent of the households have flushing toilets. According to the report, most households use a pan or a bucket for their toilet needs, and another 31.5 percent use a pit latrine.

The situation in the rural areas is even worse, with only 1.5 percent of households having access to flushing toilets. In the rural Savannahs, 69 percent have no access to toilet facilities. When it comes to sanitation, Ghana is hurting badly for a new system. Currently, according to the report, 58 percent of all households in Ghana dispose of their refuse by public dumping in pits, valleys, streams, rivers, or in the bushes somewhere. Another 8 percent of the population burns their refuse, while another 4 percent buries it (The Ghana Living Standard Survey, 2007*)*.

In a recent Supreme Court decision, Ghana has banned the use of the pan latrines, and has outlawed hand-carrying excrement in the capital city of Accra, and will be phasing this activity out during the next five years.

It has also ordered the construction of 1500 public toilets within the same time period.

## Health Issues

One fact of life in Ghana is dealing with several health issues. Malaria is a potentially fatal disease transmitted by a specific type of mosquito, the *anopheles genus*. Malaria still claims about three million lives a year, with about 90 percent of the deaths reported in Africa. Poor countries in Africa lack the means to fight malaria. Ghana had 7.2 million cases of malaria in 2007, and malaria in Ghana results in 22 percent of deaths of children under the age of five (WHO, World Malaria Report, 2010).

There are three principal ways in which malaria can contribute to death in young children. First, an overwhelming acute infection, which frequently presents as seizures or coma (cerebral malaria), may kill a child directly and quickly. Second, repeated malaria infections contribute to the development of severe anemia, which substantially increases the risk of death. Third, low birth weight which is frequently the consequence of malaria infection in pregnant women constitutes the major risk factor for death in the first month of life. In addition, repeated malaria infections make young children more susceptible to other common childhood illnesses, such as diarrhea and respiratory infections, and thus contribute indirectly to mortality.

AIDS in Ghana has also been a major problem, and has directly influenced the number of orphans in the country. In 2002, there were 330,000 people between the ages of 15-49 that were living with HIV/AIDS, and another 34,000 children between 0-14 years of age. A total of 28,000 people died in Ghana from the disease.

With all of these health situations to deal with, it only stands to reason that orphanages are not going to be ideal places to raise children. They are not going to be able to receive the type of medical treatment they need for various diseases, which run rampant through these orphanages. More children are likely to die as the problems continue inside these facilities.

While there are vast numbers of children living on the streets all over Ghana, and while extended families take care of a large proportion of orphans there, it is inevitable that the numbers of orphanages will be increasing. As grandparents reach the end of their lives, children will again be handed off to another set of family members if they have anyone else who can care for them, or they will become wards of the state, and will eventually end up in one or more orphanages.

# Economic Factors

## The Gini Index

According to some statistics, such as the Gini Index, there is a great deal of inequality that exists in Ghana. These are general measurement indicators that help determine how countries are faring around the world. The Gini Index is a standard economic measure of income inequality. A society that scores 0.0 has perfect equality of income distribution. A score of 1.0 indicates total inequality, where one person has all the income in the country.

The Gini Index can also be used to determine such things as land inequality, as well. Land inequality rates would be important to determine poverty and lifestyles in poorer countries. For example, having no land means a person is at the mercy of landowners for their jobs or food. There is more land inequality in Latin America, with Africa being very close behind.

The Gini coefficient can also help to determine and compare income distribution for different countries over time, as well. Currently, the Gini Index in Ghana is approximately .40.

## Sub-Saharan Africa

In comparing the figures in the inequality equation, other countries in Sub-Saharan Africa are much worse than Ghana. Sierra Leone, for example sits around .63, while Namibia is .70, Botswana comes in with a Gini index of .63, South Africa at .65, and Zimbabwe has an index calculated at .50.

## Fertility Rates

The term total fertility rate is used to describe the total number of children the average women in a population are likely to have based on current birth rates throughout her life (United Nations Population Division, 2009). The number ranges from more than 7 children per woman in developing countries in Africa to around 1 child per woman in Eastern European and highly-developed Asian countries.

Associated with total fertility rate is the concept of replacement rate. The replacement rate is the number of children each woman needs to have to maintain current population levels or what is known as zero population growth for her and her partner. In developed countries, the necessary replacement rate is about 2.1. Since replacement cannot occur if a child does not grow to maturity and have their own offspring, the need for the extra .1 child (a 5% buffer) per woman is due to the potential for death and those who choose or are unable to have children. In less developed countries, the replacement rate is around 2.3 due to higher childhood and adult death rates. Currently, the fertility rate in Ghana is approximately 4 children per family.

Total fertility rates are closely tied to growth rates for countries and can be an excellent indicator of future population growth or decline for a country or for a population within a country. Developed countries usually have a much lower fertility rate due to greater wealth, education, and urbanization. They also have better access to birth control. For example, the total fertility rate for the United States is just below replacement value at 2.09 and the total fertility rate for the world is 2.59, down from 2.8 in 2002 and 5.0 in 1965.

Although the *rate* of growth has been declining since the 1960s, global population grows each year by approximately 80 million people, or the equivalent of the population of a country the size of Germany. Nearly all of this growth is concentrated in the developing nations of the world, in many of which fertility rates remain high.

## Sub-Saharan Africa

As we again compare figures with some other Sub-Saharan African nations, we see the figures much higher in the region: Sierra Leone sits at 5.88 children per family, while Mali is at 7.29 children per household. Angola, Somalia, Ethiopia, and the Democratic Republic of the Congo all come in with figures over 6 children per family, while Zambia, Mozambique, Malawi all are sporting numbers of 5 or higher.

## Why Care About Fertility Rates?

High fertility can impose costly burdens on developing nations. It may impede opportunities for economic development, increase health risks for women and children, and erode the quality of life by reducing access to education, nutrition, employment, and scarce resources such as potable water. Furthermore, surveys of women in developing countries suggest that a large percentage--from 10 to 40 percent--want to space or limit childbearing but are not using contraception.

This finding indicates a continuing, unmet need for contraception. Historically, voluntary family planning programs have been very effective in filling this demand for contraception and by doing so helping developing nations to moderate high fertility rates. For example, Mexico was able to reduce its child fertility rate from just over 6, to about 4 by utilizing family planning techniques (Hicks, Johnson, & Rodriguez, 1990).

Currently, most of the world's population growth occurs in poor, developing nations, which are least able to support rapid population growth and whose socioeconomic development is most likely to be hindered by high fertility. In most of these nations, fertility rates remain high. Sub-Saharan Africa in particular has experienced less change than Asia or Latin America: Its total fertility rate is almost at 6.0, notwithstanding a downtrend in a few countries such as Kenya, Zimbabwe, Ghana, and Zambia. In Nigeria, the continent's most populous nation, the average woman will give birth to 6.5 children in her lifetime.

## The Black Star

Taking a good look at most of the statistical data on Ghana is very revealing about the country. It is poor, it has health issues, it has sanitation problems, as well as a lack of safe, potable water. However, it also served as the model for independence for the rest of Africa. Ghana was indeed a pioneer, as it became the first independent former colony in Africa on March 6, 1957. Kwame Nkrumah became the first president of Ghana, and officially changed the name to Ghana, replacing the former Gold Coast designation.

Kwame Nkruma was born in Ghana, but was educated at the University of Pennsylvania, in the United States, where he received a master's degree in education. He became one of the first African Statesmen, where he was principal in establishing Pan-Africanism. He led the country until 1966, after the United States government became dissatisfied with his socialist and communist leanings. He was later exiled, and in replaced by a dictator, but in the meantime, during his presidency, he led the way for other African countries to begin pursuing their freedom from European colonialism.

Nkruma is still highly regarded in Ghana, and his museum and memorial museum is an intellectually stimulating place to gather information and review his life.

Even today, while Ghana suffers from numerous problems, it is still attempting to rise above its dilemmas. As I began to explore the orphanage problems in Sub-Saharan Africa, I began in Ghana because it was not rife in war and conflict, and the people were accepting and friendly. While many problems will be highlighted in Ghana in later chapters, it is important to note that those problems are much worse in other parts of Sub-Saharan Africa. Today, Sub-Saharan Africa is the poorest region on earth, and its growth and development are at risk.

## Poverty in Sub-Saharan Africa

In this book, I will make references to the terms "developing world, "as well as "third world." Most of these terms are used to describe the region known as Sub-Saharan Africa. The term *Third World* was originally coined in times of the Cold War to distinguish those nations that were neither aligned with the West (NATO) nor with the East, the Communist bloc. Today the term is often used to describe the developing countries of Africa, Asia, Latin America and Oceania (World Bank Group, 2011).

The United Nations has been chiefly responsible for gathering data each year to help measure the progress of these developing nations. The Human Development Index, (HDI), for example, is published annually by the UN, and has become a chief source of information in my quest for data. The Human Development Index actually measures the average achievements in a country in three basic dimensions of human development: (1) a long and healthy life, as measured by life expectancy at birth, (2) knowledge, as measured by the adult literacy rate and the primary and secondary education levels, and (3) a decent standard of living, as measured by GDP per capita.

It's also very surprising for people to learn what is known as the "irony of poverty." In developing countries, people die from such things as hunger and not enough food, while people in the developed countries die of too much food.

When looking at such figures, it is sometimes appalling to note the differences between those third world nations and some of the richer nations, like the United States. For example, we see that the *Life Expectancy Rate at Birth* in some countries like Zambia is only 32, compared to the high 70's in most rich countries. Sierra Leone has a life expectancy of only 34. The life expectancy in Ghana is 59 for men and 61 for women.

When I was traveling in West Africa, I was amazed that everyone kept getting up and letting me have their seat on the buses, and letting me go to the front of the line in banks and other establishments. I was surprised to learn that it was because I was considered a very old man there as I was in my late fifties.

There are also those countries known as "Least Developed Countries, or LDCs." The least developed countries (LDCs) are a group of countries that have been identified by the UN as "least developed" because of the following criteria: (1) a low-income estimate of the gross national income (GNI) per capita, (2) Their weak human assets, and (3) their high degree of economic vulnerability. There are 50 countries listed in the United Nations comparative analysis of poverty: 34 African countries, 10 Asian countries, 5 Pacific Island Nations and one Caribbean nation. As we go through the sections in this book, we will find that Africa is overrepresented in several categories.

The region known as Sub-Saharan Africa is a large geographical area that lies south of the Sahara Desert. It is also known as the poorest region on earth. With a population of 800 million in 2007, it also has a population of 318 million children under the age of 18. In general, the average fertility rate in Sub-Saharan Africa is 5.7, and the under-5 mortality rate is 175 per 100,000 people. Life expectancy only reaches 48 years, and there is an adult literacy rate that stands at only 61 percent.

Currently, Sub-Saharan Africa has over 388 million people living on less than 1.25 US Dollars per day, with another 556 million individuals living on less than 2.0 US Dollars per day. Other problems also plague the rest of Africa, as we will see in later chapters.

# UNICEF

One of the most important agencies that will be considered in this study is UNICEF. *United Nations Children's Fund* was created by the United Nations General Assembly on December 11, 1946, to provide emergency food and healthcare to children in countries that had been devastated by World War II. In 1953, UNICEF became a permanent part of the United Nations System. Headquartered in New York City, UNICEF provides long-term humanitarian and developmental assistance to children and mothers in developing countries. It also provides vital statistics and reports on children in developed nations.

UNICEF works in over 150 countries, and is a global humanitarian relief organization providing children with health care and immunizations, clean water, nutrition and food security, education, emergency relief and more. Throughout this book, facts and figures about orphans, street children, and children living in poverty are largely provided through the assistance of this organization.

## Family Life and Culture in Ghana

The most significant of Ghana's major ethno-linguistic groups are the Akans of the southern and central part of the country. While the Ashanti and the Fante are very similar, culturally, the Akans are more numerous. Every Akan village has its own chief, each of which possesses their royal "stool," which denotes their power. Every chief is served by a council of elders, a body to which he must refer all important matters, and which also has the power to take the stool away if he does not perform well (Briggs, 2004). To emphasize the importance of the "chiefs" in Africa, one Ghanaian told me that when the President of the country walked into the meeting, he would bow to the chiefs, who generally outranked him in terms of importance.

The family is not only the basis of Ghanaian social organizations, but is also the main source of social security in old age (emotionally and financially) and the primary or sole caretaker for the young. The family is the basic unit of production and distribution and serves as the main agent for social control. More important, marriage continues to be the main locus of reproduction in a region where marriage is virtually universal (Van de Walle and Meekers 1994).

Studies of African societies generally indicate that within the whole sub-region, men and women are expected to marry. As a result, some researchers indicate that in Africa, marriage is nearly universal. Married life is important to many Africans, including Ghanaians, because it is the basis for assigning reproductive, economic, and noneconomic roles to individuals. Voluntary celibacy is quite rare in traditional African societies. The pro-family and marriage ideology that exists in Ghana also has implications for social relations. Among the various ethnic and linguistic groups, unmarried women are often viewed differently from the married (Takyi and Oheneba-Sakyi 1994). This may explain why by age twenty, a significant proportion of women in Ghana are married.

Since the 1960s, the Ghanaian family has come under intense stress as a result of contact with the outside world. With increasing levels of education and urbanization has come an increase in the nuclear form of marriage common in North America (Oppong 1983b). Takyi and colleagues, (2000), also found that mate selection is increasingly becoming an individual, rather than a family, matter, as it used to be.

# Changes in the Family in Ghana

The family in Ghana is currently undergoing numerous changes, as it is in other parts of Sub-Saharan Africa. Most of these changes are taking place regarding mate selection, childbearing, and property devolution. Historically, when Ghana gained its independence in 1957, there was a population of around 6 million, and has been experiencing a 4.5 percent growth rate since then. Currently, the population has risen to over 18 million.

One of the interesting observations about Ghana is that it is a "young" population. In fact, 42 percent of the population is younger than 15 years of age. While the fertility rate has remained fairly high, the life expectancy rate is rising. The life expectancy rate was only 45 years in the 1960's, and it has risen to 57.

Within the indigenous culture, families lived together, worked together, owned property together, and raised children together (Ardayfio-Shandorf, 2006). Child bearing was an important activity within the culture, and for the most part, men could have several wives. Males were typically in charge of the nuclear and extended families.

With the introduction of Christianity to Ghanaians from European cultures during the Colonial period, missionaries influenced almost all aspects of indigenous family life. What took the place of the original indigenous family was a new type of African, one who had been exposed to European ideals, while still trying to maintain Ghanaian tradition and culture. This created a state of confusion for most families in Ghana, as well as other countries in Africa. In fact, the missionaries tended to judge harshly indigenous traditions and family life. They tended to scorn such things as African music and art, dancing, systems of marriage and Ghana festivals.

# Urbanization

After colonialism, urbanization and modernization was introduced into many African societies, which further began to change families and their styles of life. For example, under the indigenous culture, elderly people were taken care of by the extended family and treated with respect and honor. Today, according to most scholars, elderly people are abandoned as young Ghanaians join the flight to the urban areas for jobs.

The family is still the principal institution in Ghana today. The family still serves a variety of functions by regulating sexual conduct and reproduction. It also serves as the main source of political power and the establishment of norms in society. It transmits culture to the young and still serves as the first line of social security for its citizens.

## Family Types in Ghana

There are basically two forms of family in Ghana: the patrilineal family that inherits from the male line and the matrilineal family that inherits from the female line. The patrilineal family is made up of a man's children, the children of his paternal brothers and sisters, his paternal grandfather, the paternal brothers and sisters of his grandfather, and the descendants of his paternal uncle in direct male line (Ardayfio-Shandorf, 2006).

The Matrilineal family is made up of a woman's children her maternal brothers and sisters, the children of her maternal sisters, her maternal grandmother, the maternal brothers and sisters of her grandmother, and the descendants of the aunts in the direct female line. Every Ghanaian is a member of one of these families. However, some people may be members of both patrilineal and matrilineal families.

Every person is a member of two families, a nuclear family and an extended family. The latter could be the customary family either parent depending on the kinship group to which the parent belongs.

There are two forms of marriage in Ghana, customary and legal. While marriage is the primary way a family is established, more than 80 percent of the marriages in Ghana are contracted under what is known as "customary law." These marriages are consummated with elaborate ceremonies, including payments and dowries. Polygyny is also allowed under customary law.

The first post-independence government tried in vain to change certain aspects of customary marriage and attempted to make monogamy the only legal form of marriage. It was defeated in parliament in 1961. However, in modern day Ghana, a man and woman can be married legally according to law, which would grant divorces and property rights. However, very few marriages are established via this route.

## The Diminishing Role of Mate Selection

The process of mate selection in Ghana has long been a function of the entire family. For example, many family members would have to approve the selection and ensure that the person was right for the family. In a traditional marriage, selecting and accepting a potential spouse is an important act, and certain conditions are approved or disapproved

(Ardayfio-Shandorf, 2006). The relatives of each party make sure that the potential spouse does not have a serious disease, and is not a criminal or a witch. They must also ensure that the potential spouse is hard-working and respectful. It is only when the families are satisfied on these points that the proposal is made or acceptance given.

In modern Ghanaian society, things are changing, however. There has been tremendous social change in the way of mate selection. While younger Ghanaians are increasing their mobility, their individualism, and their urban ways, their mate selection becomes more of an individual choice. The traditional ways of mate selection are beginning to disappear, especially in urban areas.

## Urbanization and the Strain on Families

The growth of towns and cities in Ghana has created a new stressor on families in Ghana. Modernization itself has brought about many changes in the family structure and way of life of many Ghanaians. As more and more citizens move to cities, we see the rise of many social problems. Slums are created as cities become overpopulated, giving rise to crime, juvenile delinquency and other problems, thus adversely affecting family life. With the constant change, the family tends to lose or relinquish many of its former functions. Occupational and geographical mobility and desertion are leading to broken marriages, which in turn lead to more single mother families, which in turn create more social problems for children.

## Increase in Female-Headed Households

It has been an increasing phenomenon in Ghanaian society for men to leave their homes and seek employment in mines, plantations, or to move to cities to improve their chances of finding higher-paying jobs. This has created a situation whereby there are more female-headed families. Many of these families are living in poverty as a result. Women are taking more responsibility for their children without the support of a husband

## THE HIV/AIDS Crisis and Increasing Social Problems of Children

HIV/AIDS was first reported in Ghana in 1986. Many children are being orphaned at an early age because of the concentration of the disease among the reproductive age group of the population. The care of AIDS patients is putting an increasing financial and emotional burden on affected families. This has also been a major problem throughout Sub-Saharan Africa.

In the urban areas of Ghana, a growing number of school-age children roam the streets during school hours. Most of them are from broken homes, or immigrant families whose parents are poorly employed. The orphan numbers are increasing all over Africa, especially in Sub-Saharan Africa due to a large extent on changes within the family structure, the increase of AIDS, and many other problems.

While families still represent the most important facet of Ghanaian traditional life, unfortunately, the changes that are taking place there are not positive ones. The traditions are slipping away, HIV/AIDS is chipping away at family unity, economics, education, and creating a large population of orphans.

# CHAPTER TWO

# ORPHANS:
# A GROWING PROBLEM

## Becoming an Orphan

Obviously, children become orphans for very different reasons. However, chief among the reasons can be war, child abuse, extreme poverty, or HIV/AIDS. For whatever reasons that children are orphaned, they may end up in a number of different types of facilities. Some orphanages are run by churches from other countries, and some are government operated organizations. Others may be owned and operated by unscrupulous characters that prey on children and unsuspected donors for monetary gain. In Ghana, I witnessed all three forms.

Obviously, the AIDS epidemic is going to increase the number of children who will be orphaned in the next ten years in Africa, and no one can predict where it will end (Children on the Brink, 2004). If so, orphanages will increase as well, as families struggle to take care of children they cannot afford. If nothing else, by studying the orphans and the orphanages in Africa, we can get a reasonable idea about the level of care these children are going to be experiencing, and will be able to determine if this is a viable option for those who have lost their parents.

## Families under Pressure

While the extended family remains the largest support system for orphans in Ghana and in Sub-Saharan Africa in general, that system is currently under a great amount of strain. Ninety percent of orphaned children initially end up with their extended families. This causes a greater amount of poverty for those over-burdened families. Others live with non-relatives, which may serve as foster families. In these arrangements, large numbers of children are forced to work to help provide for their own needs. In about one percent of the time, older siblings become the primary caretaker for their younger siblings.    A soaring number of orphans are also living with grandparents.

While extended families and children raising their younger siblings, there appears to be very few resources from which to draw.  For example, in America and other Western nations, there exists a safety net which would be in line to offer support and assistance.  There are foster families that have passed rigorous background checks and investigations that will provide a safe and secure home for children who have lost their parents. In most of Sub-Saharan Africa, Ghana, included, one of the major sources of support is the orphanage.

## Terminology regarding Orphans

As far as terminology is concerned, orphans have been classified into several categories by *Children on the Brink* and UNICEF. *Maternal orphans* are those children under age 18 whose mothers have died. *Paternal orphans* are those children under age 18, whose fathers have died.  *Double orphans* are those children whose mothers and fathers have died.  *New orphans* are those who have been orphans for less than a year. Other terms in the literature are *single orphans*, where only one of the parents is lost.   *New orphans* are those children under 18 who have lost one or both parents in the last year.

It is my intention to complete this research in order to better understand the problems that orphans are going through.  Emphasis will also be placed on the development of children who are living in orphanages.  As other experts have written over the years, I, too, have observed that children who grow up on the streets or in orphanages are developmentally challenged in many ways.  They become adults at early ages and the use of play is avoided or ignored all together, which may be depriving these children of vital social skills necessary for their complete development (Hollingsworth, 2008).   For example, do staff members provide enough personal touch and emotional love for the child to development a feeling of well-being?  Will they get the proper food to develop physically?  Will they be in school to develop cognitively?  What are the chances of being abused, both physically and sexually?

# Orphans in Ghana

## Prevalence

In a population of 20 million citizens, approximately 8 million of those numbers are children between 0-14 years of age. In a country with a life expectancy of only 58, there were 28,000 AIDS deaths in 2001. As of 2001, there were 759,000 orphans in Ghana, of which 204,000 are AIDS orphans (Children on the Brink, 2004). During the year 2001, there were over 326,000 maternal orphans, 509,000 paternal orphans, and 75,000 double orphans in Ghana. The 2010 projections show 734,000 orphans, which shows a slight decrease in the number of total orphans, however, when examining 2007 figures, that number of total orphans has already increased to over 1,100,000 total orphans. The numbers appear to be increasing faster than actual projections.

As far as school attendance goes, Ghana is showing a remarkable difference in attendance of non-orphans versus orphans between the ages of 10-14 years of age. Statistics show that only 72 percent of orphans that have one or more dead parents attend school.

## Sub-Saharan Africa

While the numbers of orphans varies greatly on the continent of Africa, other countries obviously have higher numbers than Ghana. For example, Cote d'Ivoire has an estimated number of 905,000 orphans as of 2002, and was expecting a slight increase by the year 2010. Other countries, such as Nigeria had over 5,421,000 orphans, with a staggering amount of 995,000 of them due to AIDS. This figure was projected to be in the neighborhood of 6.5 million by 2010.

Other staggering numbers of orphans exist in The Democratic Republic of the Congo, where 2,730,000 orphans reside, with that number increasing to well over 3 million by 2010. Other problem countries are Ethiopia, with 3,839,000 total orphans in 2001, with almost a million of them due to the AIDS epidemic. Those total numbers were also due to be hovering around 5 million in 2010. Kenya, Mozambique, Tanzania, Uganda, South Africa, and Zimbabwe are all reporting numbers exceeding one million total orphans, with all those figures expected to increase (Children on the Brink, 2004).

With such staggering numbers of orphans in Africa, how are these children faring in such facilities as orphanages? What is the quality of

their life?  What is the status of their education?  Let's take a look at some
of these orphanages in Ghana.

# First-Hand Observations of Orphanages in Ghana

## Mercy Orphanage at Teshie

It was a routine I adjusted to very quickly, and I was excited to see
firsthand how the orphans were living, and how they were being treated
inside those facilities.  We would get up in the morning, have breakfast at
the compound, and then walk several miles through dirt roads to a
Canadian-owned facility that was maintained and staffed by Ghanaians.  It
was a private facility, but well-constructed.  It was painted a bright pink on
the outside, and was surrounded by a ten foot concrete wall.  My first
thought was, "are they keeping people out, or are they keeping the orphans
in."

The building in Teshie was also a newer building, however, and they
had just moved in.  All in all, it was a nicely kept, well-constructed
facility.

As we (my co-workers and I) approached the gate for the first time, it
took a while for anyone to notice that we were there.  There were no signs
revealing the nature of the establishment.  It was located directly across
from a school.  We had to beat on the large Iron Gate until someone
finally unlocked it from the inside.  As the gate opened, we stepped into a
small courtyard where some small children were milling around.   Once
inside, we were met by the staff, which was courteous and friendly.  They
took a few minutes to show us around, which did not take long.   The
building was constructed more as a home environment than a facility to
house orphans.  Altogether, it was not an unpleasant building at all.

There were about 30 children living in the orphanage there, but there
were only two bedrooms crowded with bunk beds.  I quickly guessed,
correctly, that children were sleeping in the same bed, and that others were
sleeping on the floor at night.  There was also only one bathroom for the
children to share.  However, they did have running water, which was
considered a luxury in the Teshie area.  They had one flushing toilet and
one sink for 30 children, so the logistics of bathroom privileges were a
nightmare to say the least.

The children ranged in ages from newborn infants to thirteen years of
age.  The bulk of the children, however, were between 2 and 10.  When
the children saw us for the first time, they grabbed onto us and clung to us,

and were continuously climbing on us, begging for attention. It became very exhausting only after a few hours of being there.

## Lack of Resources

It became apparent after only a few hours that there were very few activities for the children to partake in. The living area, or the main room in the house was empty, save for a few plastic chairs and an ancient television set. Otherwise, the entire facility was void of furniture.

A VCR was set up and one of the staff put an old children's dance tape in, and the children jumped around for a while, and when the tape was over, the children just sort of wandered off. For the most part, wandering off was the main activity for these children. The staff seemed content to let the volunteers chase after the children, but also seemed ok with just letting the children wander around at will on their own.

As volunteers, we would dream up activities for the children, but we had few resources to work with. One American college girl, who had been working in the facility for a while, brought her own coloring books and crayons, and reading materials. She would gather as many of the children together as she could, and we would help them draw and color. Other times, she would read to them.

I was getting to know the children better each day, and every time I showed up, the children would come running and began climbing on me again and again. I began to engage the children in playing with a soccer ball outside, and this would keep them busy for short periods of time before they would get bored and run back inside. Their attention span appeared very small.

Each day became a challenge as to what activities we could dream up to keep the kids busy. Otherwise, they would wander the halls listlessly, crying and sobbing for no apparent reason. Even while engaging in some of the activities, some of the children would suddenly begin sobbing deep, long-lasting crying episodes. These episodes became so severe that the children would appear to lose contact with anything or anyone.

Even though the facility had a bathroom, most of the children urinated outside on the courtyard. Boys and girls would line up together and urinate along the wall that enclosed the facility. This behavior seemed to be normal, with no interference by any of the staff.

Meal times were always interesting, as the children would only get one or two meals a day. The staff would cook on a wood burning oven, which caused a large plume of smoke to emanate from the room that served as the kitchen. Soon, the entire facility would be engulfed in smoke. Most of the time, the meals consisted of rice with a little chili sauce sprinkled over the top. The children had no chairs, desks, or tables on which to eat their meals. They would sit on the floor and eat their bowl of rice quickly, then wander off again.

Their diets generally consisted of rice and cassava, both of which are very starchy and full of carbohydrates. They have very little protein in their diet, and the children all have distended abdomens from malnutrition.

After lunch, the children would be instructed to go outside and wash their bowls, which they did, reluctantly. When they returned, we would begin to come up with new activities for after lunch, which usually included storytelling, or more drawing. Sometimes, we would gather them all together and take them to the park. I quickly discovered that the trip to the park was nothing more than a dirt lot, choked with weeds, outside of a church building down the street. But, it served us well, as we took the soccer ball and some other toys with us.

Other times, we would take the children out for snacks to the local neighborhood store and buy them cookies. This was one of their favorite activities to do, as they hardly ever received any snacks from the orphanage.

Most of the children wore the same clothes day in and day out. I never saw the children wearing anything different from day to day. There seemed to be a lack of resources at the facility, especially in clothing, food, resources and activities, toys, games, books, or other items to stimulate them in any way. Even the building is stark inside, with no furniture, no decorations, no windows, and no real evidence of love, other than what the volunteers provided while they were there. Even the volunteers were in and out at irregular intervals, coming and going as they were mostly summer interns and were largely there just for the summer.

Some disturbing facts came forth as I learned that when the children turned 13, they were released from the facility. This was troublesome, as these children were completely under-prepared for living on their own, and most would have to become street children, begging for their survival. They would become vulnerable, or become victims of unscrupulous individuals, or end up as child laborers somewhere. This fact led me to investigate these other social problems, which in a way, stemmed directly from the orphans and the situations they found themselves in once they left these facilities.

I was also concerned about the lack of stimulation. For the most part, unless volunteers were there to meet their needs, the children wandered around alone, and went unsupervised by the few staff members that worked in the facility. I became concerned about their developmental needs, as well as their social, mental and physical well-being. Over the years, social scientists, medical experts, child development specialists, and social workers have been studying the patterns of child development. With 150 million orphans throughout the world, the facilities and institutions that house these children become crucial in our understanding of the development of orphans.

## The Staff at Teshie

It is interesting to note, that the staff is the primary caregiver for children who are vulnerable to certain developmental issues. Indeed, the staff becomes the most important figure in a young child's life inside these facilities. I made careful observations of the staff at Teshie, and realized that they were central to the survival of the children there, both emotionally and physically.

As I continued to work at the center at Teshie, I became more and more disillusioned. The work at the center soon became exhausting and repetitious. Day after day, there appeared to be no direct involvement by the staff. As soon as the volunteers showed up, the staff would disappear, leaving the care of the children to college students and interns. After several hours of dealing with children with their crying episodes, their numerous fights, and their temper tantrums, volunteers would become weary, and would leave in the early afternoon. I could not help but wonder how the children were treated when the volunteers would leave for the day.

While treatment from the staff was negligible during the day while the volunteers were there, some of the children complained that they were being beaten at night. Although, I never saw any marks, or other signs of violence toward the children, several children complained that the beatings occurred just before bedtime. There was never any corroborating evidence to support the claims by the children, but the incidents were all reported to IFRE officials, who claimed they would investigate.

## Lack of Medical Treatment

Other noteworthy problems in the orphanage at Teshie, was the absence of any medical treatment. Several of the children had illnesses that continued for days without medical intervention. There was no staff physician, no nursing available, and no physical checkups were available for most of the children at Teshie. It was noted that one child who was very ill, was receiving cold medicine. However, his symptoms extended into days and weeks without any change. I continued to notice this boy's runny nose and hacking cough for at least two weeks.

Obviously, the staff has few resources at their disposal. Largely, funding is hard to come by. The organization in Canada supports them in numerous ways, but the money that comes in is inconsistent. While other funding in the form of "sponsorships" is supposedly in place, it's hard to see that any of the funds are going directly to the children. For example, donations from citizens are requested by television advertisements and other methods, which claim that the money donated, will go directly to support a child to send them to school, buy clothes, and other meaningful ways. Yet, the children wear the same clothes day after day, school attendance is sparse, and the food supplies are scarce. Medicine is nonexistent, and the kids go barefoot for the most part.

While the treatment and service children received at Teshie were minimal, I understood that the lack of resources played a major role in the service provided. However, at Osu, it was a nightmare from day one.

## Observations at Osu

Osu is a district in central Accra, Ghana, known for its busy commercial, restaurant and nightlife activity. It is locally known as the 'West End' of Accra. It is also the location of the state run facility, known as the *Osu Children's Home.*

From the outside, the building appears ominous, with barbed-wire fencing across some of the area. If one did not know it was a children's center, they might mistake it for a low level prison for criminals. Personnel at the facility state that they have a complete staff of clinical psychologists, nurses, and physicians, but none of these professionals were ever seen at Osu. While I was working in Ghana, a child, age 5 died of malaria inside Osu. The only medical attention he received was some cold medicine by staff members.

They also claim that they keep the children until they are 23; however, another individual claims they only keep them until the age of 12, which is more consistent with other orphanages in the country. It appears that most orphans are released somewhere between 12 and 13 to live on their own. Children are taken into the home for various reasons, but the consensus is that they take children from parents who are serving time in prison, abandoned children, and children whose parents have died as a result of HIV/Aids.

There are four living quarters at the facility to house children, plus a nursery unit that houses children from newborns to the age of two. Three other units house children age three and above, and they are crowded together in large numbers in these units. This is a much larger institution than the one in Teshie.

The facility makes a minimal effort of enrolling children in school. At last count, of the 200 children at the facility, only 79 of the children were enrolled in school according to facility officials. What schooling they get at the facility is limited, with very few resources, very few qualified staff, and overcrowded rooms. Volunteers work with children in the schools on a regular basis.

## The Horrors of Osu Children's Home

Horror stories abound at Osu. Over 200 children were living in this facility when I was there. Children were crowded into small rooms everywhere. Rumors of staff beating children were numerous. Recently, a reporter in Ghana broke a story that got national attention concerning the Osu Children's Home. *The Crusading Guide*, an online newspaper organization in Ghana, with the aid of an undercover camera revealed troubling information regarding malicious treatment of children there (The Crusading Guide, 2008).

These stories are consistent with my own observations at the facility, and those of my colleagues who also worked in the home on a daily basis. I was able to contact the reporter, who recently has been honored by President Obama for his meritorious work in uncovering a child sex ring in Ghana. I interviewed him about the orphanage. What I learned mostly was the information that follows. He also placed footage from his hidden camera work on YouTube for the whole world to see.

The report issued by The *Crusading Guide* reveals that staff regularly beat and slapped the kids, and forced children to slap other children in the presence of the staff. One video incident shows one of the staff (staff there are called *Aunties*) telling a young boy to slap the other kid in the face. When approached by a reverend (the reporter in disguise) that saw the video, the Auntie denied the entire incident, claiming that she was not working when the incident occurred. Since that story broke, the facility has denied all the charges, which include regular beatings, rotten food, staff stealing donations made to the children, and other human rights abuses. Ghana's ace investigative journalist Anas Aremeyaw Anas in one of his undercover investigations reveals human rights abuses of the children at the Osu Children's Home at the hands of supposed care givers. Disguised as Hajia Barikisu, a merchant from Mali, Anas reveals how atrocious living conditions are inside Osu. A government spokesman in

Ghana also states that the facility is coaching the children to tell everyone that they have not been abused. The *Crusading Guide* also reports that the Police are investigating the human rights abuses at the facility.

While I was there, I observed definite marks on children which would corroborate beatings, as well as other mistreatment. I personally witnessed staff taking donations that were meant for the children. This became a common incident as I discussed this matter with my colleagues who worked in the facility.

One final note about Osu, was that all the volunteers have recently been denied access to the facility, according to the press, as the officials at Osu are blaming volunteers for leaking the human rights abuses to the press, which may have prompted the undercover operation. This is also a tactic to keep outsiders from reporting on what they see at the facility. My observations at the facility could do nothing more than corroborate what Anas Aremeyaw Anas has reported.

## Other orphanages in Ghana

As I made my way around Ghana, trying to observe as many orphanages as I could, I also interviewed other volunteers who had been working in several other orphanages there. One in particular was a facility called *Sachabu* in Vakpo, Ghana. This facility, as you approach it from the outside, looks normal, but once inside, the observer is amazed at what they are actually calling an orphanage. It is a brown, dismal-looking frontage from the outside, and on the inside, it takes on the appearance of a bombed out building, with no roof, and no furniture to speak of. Approximately 60 children live in this facility.

## Lack of Resources/Hazards

The children are herded into their makeshift school rooms during the day, which contains no resources or materials. Teachers actually use chalk to write on concrete walls because there are no chalk boards. Classrooms are small concrete rooms with no furniture, and only one teacher was available at any given time. As in other orphanages I had visited Most of the work was done by volunteers at the facility.

Play areas were outside on dirt and gravel, and the grounds were littered with glass and other hazardous debris. Sanitation was also a problem, as children urinated and defecated in the play area on a regular basis. Clean water is a problem there, as well, and it has been noted that there is one bucket of clean water for the children, and they all use the same cup to drink out of.

Clearly, there was no governmental regulation at this facility, and health care was a major concern. Other orphanages in the country were just as bad, if not worse. There was one particular orphanage near Teshie that claimed that they were an orphanage, and they were in the process of obtaining more children. Every time the volunteers would report there for their work shifts, the owner would ask them for money. The building had no roof, and no furniture, and the owner was eventually barred from using IFRE volunteers later for his scheming tactics.

Africa has a major problem addressing the huge orphan population. Ghana is just one country that is experiencing these difficulties. Orphanages in other African countries are facing similar conditions, with harsh treatment of the children, lack of resources, unscrupulous administration, corruption, staff problems, and minimal education of its residents. Lack of sanitation is also a problem all through Africa, and it is no different for orphanages. There is a lack of clean drinking water, lack of medical attention, and diseases such as malaria still plague Africa. All of these problems affect children that are living in these facilities.

When absolute poverty is the order of the day for most African communities, it is bound to affect the conditions inside orphanages, as well. If the staff are taking donations home with them that are supposed to be reaching the orphans, what does that say about the living conditions of the staff that are employed in those facilities?

## Developmental Needs of Orphans

One of the chief concerns about orphans is the need for continual development. Once a child's parents die, a child's full potential is seriously threatened. According to most research, to survive and thrive, children and adolescents need to grow up in a family and community environment that provides for their changing needs, thereby promoting their healthy and sound development (Children on the Brink, 2004).

Depending on the age of the child, and their current levels of physical, cognitive, emotional, and psychosocial development, they will experience this death in different ways. Infants under five years of age are the most vulnerable, obviously, as they need to feel attached to a maternal figure early on in their development.

John Bowlby, in his early studies in the 1950's, observed that delinquent boys had suffered early maternal separation and concluded that a strong mother-child bond is essential to psychological well-being

(Bowlby, 1956). He warned against separating children from their mothers, and his theory of attachment became an important work. According to Bowlby, one of the goals infants seek is attachment to other humans, generally to the primary caregiver, that is, the person who takes charge of caring for the child. Since mothers are the first to have a long-term association with the child, the first and perhaps most important attachment figure is the child's mother.

When a young child loses such a caregiver, he or she is at risk of losing the ability to make close emotional bonds. Long-term institutional care is particularly inappropriate, as those infants consistently need to form bonds with a consistent care giver. In orphanages, this attachment is lost. At best, the staff may act as care givers, but at an inconsistent rate. Even volunteers, who become short term caregivers, come and go quickly, leaving children confused and lost.

## Crying Episodes

Young children learn best when they feel safe, calm, protected, and nurtured by their caregivers. When a child's attachment process is disrupted, the child's brain will focus on meeting its survival needs and abandon the emotional and cognitive growth. The crying episodes I described earlier may have been a survival tactic that the child manufactured to feel safe. These crying episodes which would appear out of nowhere, and last for hours at times, seemed to completely possess the children, and they would pull deep within themselves, becoming non-communicative and unresponsive. It's quite possible that at that level, they had physically and mentally retreated to their own manufactured safe zone. The children that I observed with these crying episodes were between two and five years of age, where they would have been most vulnerable to a lack of attachment.

Erik Erikson (1902-1994), a German-born psychoanalyst who studied at the Vienna Psychoanalytic Institute before coming to the United States, produced monumental work regarding human development as he improved on Sigmund Freud's work, who was one of the first scientists to concentrate on child development. Erikson concentrated on the nature of a healthy personality and of ego identity, as well as today's most accepted ideas of psychosocial growth.

Erikson suggested that a sense of trust, or being able to predict and depend upon one's own behavior and the behavior of others, is derived primarily from the experiences of the first year of life (Erikson, 1950). In other words, a child's fundamental attitude about the dependability of the world is built chiefly on the relationship established as an infant during the stage when feeding is of prime importance. The most important person in the infant's life at this juncture is the mother, or the mother substitute. A disruption at this stage, according to Erikson, would create a psychosocial crisis in the form of *mistrust*.

The children at the orphanage that had engaged in the crying episodes were usually between the ages of 2 and 4, and had spent the first years of their lives at the facility already. It is entirely feasible to believe that these children were already facing their first crisis in their young lives: mistrust. The children appeared to be withdrawing within them to a place no one else could enter.

Middle Childhood has its own precarious developmental issues. Middle childhood, according to experts, begins around the time a child enters primary school. As children of this age group face new developmental challenges, the experience of serious parental illness or death, affects them differently than infants and younger children.

Orphans at this stage of development are able to understand the concept of death, but may have other issues, such as fear of abandonment and loss. They may experience forms of anxiety at times, with bouts of regression to a younger behavior. One important concept at this stage of development, school attendance, becomes essential for them to continue their level of development. According to Erikson, a child who does not develop well during those school years may develop a sense of inferiority and inadequacy.

## Lack of Education and Development

It was interesting to note, that while school at this age is almost essential for normal childhood development, very few of the children at the orphanages I observed attended school on a regular basis. Most of the children of school age at the orphanage at Teshie stayed at the orphanage all day, associating with the volunteers and other children that were younger. Some of the older kids, mostly adolescents did attend school, but the younger children did not. Orphans in Africa often miss out on opportunities to go to school, while others are subjected to substandard school rooms with few resources or classrooms that were inadequate.

## The Disadvantages of Being Orphaned

There are several devastating outcomes for children who have been orphaned. Initially, there are cognitive, emotional, as well as social development issues to contend with (Children on the Brink, 2004). When children are orphaned as a result of AIDS, there is the additional trauma of losing their parents. Other problems soon may develop, such as a lack of education, or the increase in child labor. For those extended families that take on the responsibilities of taking in orphans, there is the added economic burden, which increases the likelihood of growing up in poverty.

Orphans are more likely to have their schooling interrupted, as well. Studies in Kenya, Zimbabwe, and the United Republic of Tanzania show that the probability of being at the proper education level is worse for orphans who have lost one or more parents, compared to non-orphans.

Child labor is another chief concern among orphaned children. Studies in Sub-Saharan Africa show a high proportion of children working than any other region, with 29 percent of the children working, especially as parents die from HIV/AIDS. It becomes necessary for them to enter the work force to survive. Some studies, however, show that their occupations are less than acceptable activities for children. Some studies have, in fact, suggested that some children are engaging in prostitution. A rapid assessment by Children on the Brink in Zambia also found that the average age of children engaged in prostitution was 15. Forty-seven percent of these children were double orphans and 24 percent were single orphans.

When orphanages release children at the age of 13 or 14, the children have no place to go, so the possibilities of becoming street children increase. This also leads directly to orphans becoming vulnerable. Once they hit the streets, they can remain at the mercy of such things as child labor, child sex trafficking, child soldiering, and other major social problems. Sub-Saharan Africa has become a hotbed for these activities, and will be dealt with in later chapters.

## Lack of Regulation and Supervision

One of the most important facts about orphanages in most developing nations is that they are lacking in essential services, resources, qualified staff, and even food and medical supplies. However, one area that may even be more important than resources is regulation and supervision of institutions.

One individual in Ghana was receiving volunteers from IFRE, and had occupied an abandoned building in the Teshie area. He began by accepting children on a temporary child care basis, but very quickly began to call it an orphanage. He had no money, no supplies, no experience, and no one knew anything about him. Within days of opening, he was already being investigated by IFRE for child abuse, stealing donated items, and trying to extort money from volunteers.

Today, there is a lack of regulation of current orphanages, and those who want to start up an orphanage can do it on a whim, with no criminal background checks, no quality control standards, or sufficient resources. This creates a dangerous system in which children can be used as child laborers, or can be exploited by child sex trafficking rings.

My experiences in Ghana's orphanages were an eye-opening affair. On one hand, I sympathized with the burden the facilities were taking on, but at the same time, I realized that they were doing a poor job of maintaining developmental standards for the children that were located there.

In effect, these children become "invisible" to mainstream Ghanaian society once they reach the orphanages. If the families can't take orphans in, they are doomed to a life of hardship and disadvantages. They will not receive a proper education which will restrict their skill set once they become an adult. In fact, most of the orphans that are released from those institutions are in for a life of living on the street, becoming criminals, or becoming involved in reprehensible situations. However, one of the problems in Africa is the education system itself. Even for children that are not orphans, the education system in Sub-Saharan Africa is lacking.

# CHAPTER THREE

# LACK OF EDUCATION

I was walking down a street in Ghana, West Africa, one day, not too far away from our compound, when I passed a rundown building on a side street. I passed two Ghanaian women who were standing on the sidewalk. When they saw me and my two female friends, they began chattering loudly at us.

"Are you Americans?" They asked excitedly.

We all responded that we were. They became even more excited. They continued to ask what we did for a living. My two friends were college undergraduates, and myself, a college professor at a liberal arts University in Texas.

"Please come inside and teach our students," they said, rather sadly. "We have no teachers for our school."

I did not know it was a school. From all outward appearances, it looked more like a warehouse. Everywhere I went in Ghana, such requests were made. Even in schools that had teachers, I could not help but notice that the classrooms were nothing less than mayhem. They were terribly overcrowded, with rooms full of children that were noisy and bored. They would run out of their classrooms to yell at us as we would pass by without a word from their teachers. One would get the impression that it was not a good learning environment.

## Millennium Development Goals and Education

One of the chief concerns about children in developing countries is the lack of quality education. The Millennium Development Goals (MDGs) are eight international development goals that all 192 United Nations members states and at least 23 international organizations have agreed to achieve by the year 2015. They include eradicating extreme poverty, reducing child mortality rates, fighting disease epidemics such as AIDS, and developing a global partnership for development. Number two on the list was to "achieve universal primary education."

# What are the Numbers?

UNICEF estimates that over 100 million children of primary school age were out of school in 2008, worldwide.  Looking at figures from around the world's developing regions, UNICEF reports indicate that South Asia has the highest number of out-of-school children at 33 million.  These numbers are followed by West and Central Africa with 25 million, and Eastern and Southern Africa with another 19 million children out of school.   Sub-Saharan Africa, however, if counted as one geographic region, leads the world with only 65 percent of primary-age children in school (UNICEF, *Progress for Children*, 2010).

According to the United Nations, there is some concern about reaching those millennium development goals.  According to their own reports, they feel that the goals will not be reached by the desired year of 2015.  Achieving universal primary education actually means keeping children enrolled continuously.  That objective has not been met, either.  In fact, the dropout rate is horrendous in Sub-Saharan Africa.  More than 30 percent of the children will drop out before reaching a final grade.  According to experts at UNICEF, Sub-Saharan Africa will need more than double the number of teachers they currently have in order to meet the target goal by 2015.

# The African Situation

Countries in Africa are in trouble with their numbers that are enrolled in school, such as Ethiopia with only 45 percent of their children attending primary school, and only 27 percent ever reaching secondary school.  In Madagascar, only 19 percent of the children attend secondary school.  Burkina Faso is another West African country that is not educating their children, with only 47 percent attending primary school, and only 12 percent reaching secondary school.  Chad has only 10 percent of its children in secondary school.  Somalia may be the worst place on the planet for educating children, with only 23 percent of their children in primary schools, and less than 7 percent in Secondary school attendance (UNICEF, 2010).

There were 17 countries with more than 500,000 out-of-school children in 2009, according to UNESCO (*The United Nations Educational, Scientific and Cultural Organization)* statistics. Nine of these countries are located in sub-Saharan Africa. Nigeria alone was home to almost 9 million out-of-school children or 37% of its primary school-age population in 2007.  Ethiopia had the second highest number of out-of-school children in the region at 2 million in 2009. This represents 16 percent of the country's primary school-age population, which nevertheless reflects considerable progress since 1999, when the figure reached 63% (UNESCO, 2011).

Many other sub-Saharan African countries have managed to significantly reduce their numbers of out-of-school children during the last decade. Between 1999 and 2009, the share of out-of school children declined by more than 30 percentage points in Burundi, Madagascar, Mali, Mozambique, Niger and the United Republic of Tanzania. Much of this progress has been due to the abolishment of school fees. Even so, the proportion of children out of school is still very high in the following countries: Equatorial Guinea (46%), Côte d'Ivoire (43%), Niger (41%), Burkina Faso (36%) and the Central African Republic (31%).

In most industrialized and First World countries, school officials have a built-in system of compulsory education. Most jurisdictions have truant officers who are in place to ensure children go to school. If parents don't educate their children, they can be held accountable in a variety of ways. While attendance at schools in Africa may be compulsory on the surface, the realities are that it is almost impossible to enforce, and because the culture is so different, compulsory attendance regulations are mostly ignored.

## Why is Education in Africa so Difficult?

In some countries, education of children is an expensive undertaking. In some developing countries, families cannot afford to send their children to school. Only the richer families can afford this luxury. School uniforms are required in most developing countries, and other things, like books and school supplies are too expensive for most poor families.

A lack of funding may also exist in order to hire qualified teachers. In some African countries, where HIV/AIDS has run rampant, there is a shortage of qualified professionals, such as teachers. Teachers may be volunteers who only work a part of the year, or may be adults who lack a proper education themselves.

In Ghana, as stated at the outset of this chapter, when I was there working in orphanages, we often would be flagged down by school officials who were standing outside the buildings, and would ask us to come and teach their students. Many of my friends would volunteer daily at some of these schools, as qualified teachers were lacking. Many of these volunteers were college students, volunteering whenever they could do so.

Other societies do not believe in educating girls. When looking at the figures from the UNICEF report, in most developing countries, it is boys who generally receive most of the education. Girls are sometimes seen as second class citizens, suitable only for procreation and nurturing their families. This is particularly true in most Sub-Saharan African countries.

The problem with education in poorer countries is not only a lack of funding for education, but also a lack of infrastructure. While basic education may be mandatory in many countries, the quality of education is far from adequate. As the educational demands around the industrialized nations increase, the developing world is falling even farther behind.

## Consequences of the Lack of Education

The lack of education in the developing world means more than just another generation of illiterate children, who will enter into the same cycle as their parents. This is a generation of children who will continue into a life of poverty, with no real tools to fight the cycle that plagues their families and villages. The agency of the United Nations that gathers the most statistics on education in third world countries is UNESCO.

## Cultural and Family Variations

Children do not go to school, or our pulled from school, for a number of reasons. However, the largest reason, is that children are used to assist the families and work. It must be clearly understood that while many children are forced to work in horrid child labor conditions, much of which is child slavery, many are working alongside their families in the fields or home (UNESCO, Global Monitoring Report, 1998).

In most situations, African children often work and go to school (Kielland & Tovo, 2006). Conversely, in an American or Westernized nation, this is quite often the reverse. Western society expects children to go to school, not work. Often, in Sub-Saharan Africa, school is reserved for those who can afford it. The richer the parents, the more likely children will attend school.

Most families in Sub-Saharan Africa may ask themselves three questions about their children going to school (Kielland & Tovo, 2006). What would children do if they didn't go to school? Who will do their work if they go to school? What will schooling do for the children and for the family? In most Western cultures, these questions would never be asked to begin with.

In Africa, particularly, according to a UNESCO report, education systems in the region reflect differences in geography, cultural heritage, colonial history, and economic development progress. The impact of French, English, and other countries' colonial policies toward education has had a lasting impact on the objectives, structure, management, and financing of education systems in the region. When African countries gained independence from colonial rule around 1960, the region lagged far behind other regions on nearly every education indicator.

## Economic Crisis

The economic crisis of the 1980s severely affected education in Africa. Declining public resources and private economic hardship resulted in an erosion of quality and primary level participation rates. As of the early twenty-first century, these setbacks have not yet been reversed. At every level, education facilities are too few, while those that exist are often in poor repair and inadequately equipped.

Teachers are often underpaid and under qualified and rarely receive the support and supervision they need to do an effective job. The number of hours spent in the classroom by most African students is far lower than the international standard. Instructional materials are often in desperately short supply. Not surprisingly, learning achievement is almost always far below the instructional objectives specified in the curricula. While country experiences vary a great deal, the reality for too many Africans is one of education systems characterized by low quality and limited access (UNESCO, 2010).

In almost all countries, access has expanded far too slowly to achieve international education targets for gender equity and universal primary education. About 12 percent of the world's children aged six to eleven live in Africa, yet the region accounts for more than one-third of the world's out-of-school children. Unless these trends reverse, Africa will account for three-quarters of out-of-school children by 2015.

Sub-Saharan African countries increased their real expenditure on education by more than 6% each year over the past decade, according to a new report published by UNESCO. Yet despite these investments, many countries in the region are still a long way from providing every child with a quality primary education (UNESCO, 2010).

## Poverty Factors

Participation problems are exacerbated by the absence of an environment for effective learning. Children are taught in overcrowded classrooms by under qualified and frequently unmotivated teachers who are often poorly and irregularly paid and receive little managerial support. Teacher absenteeism is widespread, disrupting learning and eroding public confidence in the value of public education. Shortages of learning materials further constrain learning. In ten of eleven countries surveyed by UNESCO, more than one-third of the students had no chalkboards in their classrooms. In eight countries, more than half of the students in the highest grade had no math books. Most African children spend roughly half the time in the classroom that children in other countries do (UNESCO, *Association for the Development of Education in Africa*, 2001).

When I was working in the orphanages in West Africa in which there were school rooms, there were no school supplies at all. The teachers were harsh in their presentation, used physical violence against children in the classroom, and had no blackboards, chalk, or other resources. In one orphanage school in *Sachabo*, the teachers would write on concrete walls with limestone rocks because they had no chalk board and no chalk.

Poverty-related deprivation further contributes to low educational attainment in Africa. Poor children spend more time than other children contributing to household work. As a result they are less likely to spend out-of-school hours on schoolwork, more likely to be absent from school during periods of peak labor demand, and more likely to be tired and ill-prepared for learning when they are in the classroom (UNESCO, 2001).

## War and Conflict

War and violent conflict in Africa is perhaps one of the greatest education challenges. Regions in Africa that have constantly been involved in war and conflict causes poverty, inequality, and children and the educational systems are often affected greatly (UNESCO, 2011). Armed conflict is robbing 28 million children of an education by exposing them to widespread rape and other sexual violence, targeted attacks on schools and other human rights abuses.

For example, according to the latest statistics by UNESCO, in conflict-affected African countries, 28 million primary school children are out of school. This amounts to about 42 percent of the world's total. The worst case scenario, however, is that money that ordinarily could be spent on education gets diverted into military spending.

Social and economic progress in Africa will depend to a large extent on the scope and effectiveness of investments in education. If living standards are to be raised, sustained efforts will be needed to narrow the gaps in educational attainment and scientific knowledge between Africa and other regions and to bridge the digital divide. Decades of research and experience in Africa and elsewhere have shown the pivotal role of a well-educated population in initiating, sustaining, and accelerating social development and economic competitiveness. Numerous studies show that education, particularly primary education, has a significant positive impact on economic growth, earnings, and productivity.

According to UNESCO reports (2011), there are number of facts and figures that need to be observed. In fact, in conflict and war zones in Africa, currently, statistics show that the educational system is facing numerous problems educating children. For example, children in conflict-affected poor countries are twice as likely to die before their fifth birthday as children in other poor countries. Other statistics show that only 79% of young people are literate in conflict-affected poor countries.

In fact, the world's 43 million refugees and internally displaced people have limited access to education: In 2008, just 69% of primary school age refugee children in UNHCR camps were attending primary school. In addition, twenty-one developing countries are currently spending more on arms than on primary schools – if they were to divert just 10% of military spending to education, they could put an additional 9.5 million children into school.

## Child Labor and Education Factors

As I proceeded to investigate and observe schools in Western and Sub-Saharan Africa, it became obvious that there were many factors as to why children are not being educated there. Child labor seemed to be one of the most important elements to consider, outside of the facts mentioned earlier, such as living in a war zone, or going to sub-standard schools. There is a cultural element involved that takes prominence, and that is the link between child labor in Africa, and the lack of education.

Most demand for child labor comes from the child's own household (Kielland & Tovo, 2006). Culturally speaking, if a family has assets such as cattle or a farm, the greater the need for child labor, thus the debate about whether a child will even attend school would take on much importance. Families must also weigh the advantages against the disadvantages of school attendance.

While it would seem important that having educated children in society would lead to an improvement in many areas in Sub-Saharan African society, if a family's well-being is going to be sacrificed by a child attending school, it would not be reasonable to expect them to attend school. When weighing the evidence, the quality of education in most places in Africa, must be analyzed as to the worthiness of school attendance for children. Therefore, child labor becomes a major element for examination in Sub-Saharan African societies.

# CHAPTER FOUR

# CHILD LABOR

## Prevalence: How bad is it?

In its Global Report on child labor, (2010), the International Labor Organization (ILO) has said that the global number of child laborers had declined from 222 million to 215 million, or 3 per cent, over the period 2004 to 2008, representing a "slowing down of the global pace of reduction." The report also expressed concern that the global economic crisis could "further brake" progress toward the goal of eliminating the worst forms of child labor by 2016.

The International Labor Organization was created in 1919, as part of the Treaty of Versailles that ended World War I, to reflect the belief that universal and lasting peace can be accomplished only if it is based on social justice. The Constitution was drafted between January and April, 1919, by the Labor Commission set up by the Peace Conference, which first met in Paris and then in Versailles.

The Commission, chaired by Samuel Gompers, head of the American Federation of Labor (AFL) in the United States, was composed of representatives from nine countries: Belgium, Cuba, Czechoslovakia, France, Italy, Japan, Poland, the United Kingdom and the United States. It resulted in a tripartite organization, the only one of its kind bringing together representatives of governments, employers and workers in its executive bodies.

Much of the information obtained about child labor comes from the ILO, including definitions, descriptions, and prevalence. One of the most important issues today is a form of child labor known as the "Worst Forms" of child labor. This chapter will examine child labor known chiefly as subsistence child labor, or child labor in and around the household, and child labor for economic necessity, such as commercial labor, and apprenticeships. The Worst Forms of child labor will be discussed in later chapters.

## The Idealization of the Culture of Childhood

While we typically view a child to be defined as someone under the age of 18, we also tend to universalize what a child is expected to do and become when they are under the age of 18. Childhood in Western culture currently consists of play, fun activities, and being free from adult chores and duties. In most Western countries, children typically go to school until they reach a certain age, and then are expected to prepare for adulthood by a number of different methods. For example, college or careers are expected to begin, followed soon by marriage and parenthood. However, this has not always been the case.

Childhood has not always been viewed as described above. In fact, the whole concept of childhood is a social construct that may vary according to region, class, and cultural differences (Mintz, 2010). Historically, over the past four centuries, almost all aspects of childhood and expectations have changed. Societal views over punishment, discipline, and participation in work have also changed.

In Colonial America, for example, a parent's duty was to hurry a child toward adult status as soon as possible. The goal was to get children speaking, reading, reasoning, and contributing to their family's economic well-being as quickly as possible (Mintz, 2010). Urban working class children often contributed to the family economy through scavenging, collecting wood, coal, or other items. Children also worked in the streets selling products to help supplement the family income.

## Child Labor in America

It is interesting to note, than in the United States of America, we have not always guaranteed an easy childhood, void of child labor. In fact, child labor laws were not clearly established in the U.S. until the 1930's, with the help of Lewis Hines and the child labor movement that called for regulations and laws against the exploitation of American children. For decades, in the U.S., children have worked to support their families, slaving away in coal mines, factories, or other labor intensive endeavors, often for 12 hours a day, and for very little money.

Children also worked in sweatshops in New York City's garment district, working long hours and getting paid very little to sew clothes. According to the U.S. Census in 1880, 1,118,000 children (all under the age of 16) were a regular part of the American workforce. Lewis Hine called attention to this problem in America when he began photographing these working children for the National Child Labor Committee in the early 1900's.

His investigative work revealed that there were working children all over America being exploited by American companies. In fact, many of these children lived in poverty, never went to school, and had no real home. In New York City, alone, thousands of homeless working children lived in shelters run by the Children's Aid Society. Interestingly enough, most Americans respected these children as enterprising youngsters who were doing everything to help their families, or to support themselves.

In mining areas, boys as young as ten began working in the pits as breakers, separating coal from slate and wood. Farm labor, especially, was a source of work for children, as they were out pulling weeds, milking cows, and feeding chickens. Even school attendance varied a great deal (Mintz, 2010).

It wasn't until the 1920's and 30's that the field of child psychology emerged, and had a major impact on parenting and child development. Today, we no longer see childhood as something to "rush through," rather we see it as a formative stage for later life. We believe that a child's experiences during the first two or three years of life mold their personalities. We also believe that development proceeds through a number of physical, psychological, social, and cognitive stages.

## Importance of Play on Social Development of Children

Several key figures have written about the importance and functions of play among children. For example, Erik Erickson (1950) believed that play permitted the child to work off past emotions and to find imaginary relief for past frustrations. Because these tensions are relieved in play, the child or adult is better able to cope with problems in life and to work efficiently. Thus, psychoanalytic theorists believe play permits an individual to let off excess physical energy, and to release pent-up tensions.

Jean Piaget (1962), a prominent theorist who studied cognitive development in children viewed play as a medium to help children advance their ability to learn to think properly. Play, according to Piaget allows children to practice their competencies and acquired skills in a relaxed, pleasurable way.

Other developmental experts also have agreed that play is a way for the child to safely explore and seek out new information. Daniel Berlyne (1960) saw play as exciting and pleasurable in itself because it satisfied the exploratory drive of individuals. Other researchers have observed children at play and categorized the different methods in which children carry on the function of play.

## Different Types of Play

Perhaps the most elaborate attempt to examine developmental changes in children's social play was conducted many years ago by Mildren Parten (1932). Based on observations of children in free play at nursery school, she developed several different categories of play. According to Parten, there is unoccupied play, solitary play, onlooker play, parallel play, associative play, as well as cooperative play. Each of these forms of play satisfies a different developmental focus for children, and contributes to their overall development of social skills.

## Functions of Play

According to these developmental experts, play is an important and vital part of a child's life. It is thought to increase interaction and cooperation with other children, allowing them to practice social roles they will follow later in life. Play may also allow a release of anxiety and tension, as well as advancing cognitive development in children.

## A Presumption of Childhood

In North America, there also exists a preconceived notion that I will call the *"presumption of childhood."* That is, we hold the concept of childhood sacred, and we believe that childhood itself is a designated period of social and intellectual development where children can relax and play and partake in games (Hollingsworth, 2008). This, in turn helps them develop, socially and cognitively. I first put this term into effect in *Children of the Sun: an Ethnographic Study of Street Kids of Latin America*, (2008), while working and observing street children behavior in Peru and Mexico.

Children in Sub-Saharan Africa suffer the same fate, at an earlier timeframe in their social, cognitive, and physical development. They begin work at early ages, mainly to support the family economically. This turns them into early adults, or what I term "pseudo-adults," just as the street children do in Latin America. Childhood in western societies lasts roughly through the first twelve years of life. It is also a period characterized by freedom from responsibilities. In fact, childhood is far from just being an issue of biological maturation. In fact, the existence of a predetermined childhood that contains fun and games may not be an automatic activity for children of some cultures today. In cultures where poverty exists, for example, play may not be guaranteed at all. For children who live in poverty the first 12 years of life may be a period marked by work or other adult activity. This becomes especially true in the region of Sub-Saharan Africa; therefore, an analysis of culture is in order before any assumptions can be made about the region.

# A Cultural Analysis of Child Labor

## Socialization of Child Labor

Most African children start working at early ages. According to most scholars, by the time children reach three or four years old, they are expected to work in the household on a regular basis (Kielland & Tovo, 2004). The work is expected to enhance their way of life. For example, children may be sent to fetch fire wood, or perform such menial chores as they are capable. Work on the family farm is expected and understood.

## The Age Factor

Most of the Westernized world has tried to universalize what is considered to be a child. In almost all respects, there seems to be a universal standard that rates the age of children as someone who is under the age of 18. However, this age consideration can be seen as questionable in Sub-Saharan Africa where a person is regarded as an adult once they have completed a "rite of passage" ceremony, regardless of biological age. Owing to this definitional gap, we have a problem applying the world "child" to all those under 18 in Sub-Saharan Africa. This also becomes a factor when defining "child soldiers," as well (Wessells, 2006).

# Typical Child Labor in Sub-Saharan Africa

## Household Work and Family Subsistence

In certain parts of Sub-Saharan Africa, work becomes a way of life. For example, herding animals becomes the mainstay of their lifestyle from early ages. This type of labor is common in such countries as Botswana, where children will guard herds of cattle, thus placing themselves at risk for encounters with snakes and predators. Unfortunately, most children will spend more time with cows than school books (Kielland & Tovo, 2004).

Fetching water may be one of the most important and most frequent types of child labor all over Sub-Saharan Africa. It is not uncommon to see children walking with buckets on their heads, walking to the nearest water source. I witnessed this on a daily basis in Ghana. In some rural areas, fetching water is daunting work, as the nearest source of water may be miles away.

Other activities expected by the families is doing dishes. While this sounds somewhat benign, it is good to understand that since most families do not have running water, washing dishes means toting the dishes down to the nearest water sources and cleaning them there. This become very tedious and labor intensive work.

Looking at numbers around different parts of Sub-Saharan Africa, one can quickly realize that child labor is not the exception; it is the rule (Kielland & Tovo, 2004). One study by the United Nations Development Programme (UNDP) in Benin carried out a unique time allocation study on child labor. While the study revealed a 27.5 percent participation rate, the study concluded that almost all of the 6-14 year olds in the sample did in fact carry out some sort of work during the 24 hours they were under observation.

## What is Considered Child Labor?

The ILO defines child labor in accordance with the Minimum-Age Convention as:

- For 5-11 year olds: "All children at work in economic activity." ILO does not define household chores in one's own household as being economic activity.
- For 12-14 year olds: "All children at work in economic activity, minus those in light work. Light work is defined as nonhazardous work, for up to fourteen hours a week. Hazardous work, in turn, is any activity or occupation that can lead to adverse effects on the child's safety, health, and moral development.
- For 15-17 year olds: "All children in the 'worst forms of child labor." The unconditional worst forms are, according to ILO Convention 182: slavery, trafficking, bondage, serfdom and forced compulsory labor, child soldiering, child prostitution, and use of children in drug smuggling and other criminal activities. In addition comes "work which, by its nature or the circumstances in

which it is carried out, is likely to harm the health, safety or morals of children."

## Types of Child Labor in Sub-Saharan Africa

Since work is considered such a common activity in Sub-Saharan Africa, let's examine some of the most common forms of work that children are participating in. There are several typologies when observing child labor.

### Subsistence Agriculture

One of the most common forms of child labor common in Africa is subsistence agriculture. Families farm together in a constant struggle for survival. Farming, thus, becomes a common form of their lifestyle, creating a strong feeling of solidarity and togetherness (Kielland & Tovo, 2004).

It is expected that children will work on the family farm, and in turn, are learning techniques and knowledge that will aid in their future survival. Such work might include staying up at night, keeping elephants from trampling through their crops, and scaring birds away. It is not only normal but also suitable that children work on the family farm. According to most scholars, when a household possesses large amounts of land, cattle, or other labor-intensive work, children are more likely to be engaged in labor.

According to some estimates, over 80 percent of Africa child labor is related to subsistence agriculture. The more farmland a peasant family has, the more likely the children of the household will work. Of course, this lifestyle has a direct effect on their education. Most of these children are not in line with going to school daily, although some may go part time. It becomes more important to work and help support the family.

### Apprenticeships

One of the most important things children can do in Sub-Saharan Africa is to try and establish an apprenticeship. This is important, because learning a trade can be just as valuable as going to school. To learn a craft would eventually lead to a better future, so some children may enter into work agreements for these purposes.

However, like school, apprenticeships may only be reserved for those families who can afford to lose a child laborer within their own environments. In this regard, if a family can swing it, their child may enter into a contract to a skilled merchant and learn such trades as carpentry, mechanics, and tailoring.

In Ghana, every morning I would go out running with a partner down to the end of the fishing village in which I was living at Teshie. As the sun was coming up over the Atlantic, I would see children leaving to meet their fishing boats for a long day at work. I also witnessed numerous young boys at Cape Coast on the Coast of Ghana working on the docks, fishing for private and commercial boats, spending long hours and enduring harsh conditions for very little, if any pay. These types of jobs were considered apprenticeships, where the child was learning an actual trade.

In some regards, children working as apprentices on fishing boats are treated more as slaves than trainees. Around the Lake Volta area in Ghana, it has been common to see children working in extreme conditions in the fishing business. Some NGO's in the area have even described physical abuse of young boys, and harsh treatment with no pay. Some children report that being "fed" was their only pay.

To learn a craft is the dream of some children, as their schooling has not paid off in any form of economic success. Therefore, learning a trade such as fisherman, or tailor, or mechanic, is a way to earn a living. Sometimes, families will pay a person to teach their child a trade. Considering the quality of education in Sub-Saharan Africa, it seems that a child would probably fare better learning a trade than depending on an education. Other such apprenticeships exist, as well, such as the fashion industry, hairdressing, and the construction business.

## Observations of Cape Coast Children in Ghana

There are two very important tourist spots in Cape Coast: Elmina, and the Cape Coast Castles. Both are former slave dungeons occupied by Portuguese and British slavers involved in the Atlantic Slave Trade. Lurking outside on the grounds are groups of children working and hustling tourists for money. These are children who are working, attempting to make money for their families.

Most of these children are young adolescents, approximately 12-14 years of age. Most still live with their families, but some are actually orphans and street children trying to make money the best way they know how. Most of them attempt to go to school, and juggle their work schedules at the castles.

I interviewed a number of these working children while visiting the Cape Coast area, and found some interesting information about them. One child in particular was 12 years old, and he insisted on taking my picture in front of the castle. At one point, he managed to make me drop my camera, thereby, breaking it. He felt bad, and then offered to be my personal guide at Cape Coast. The young boy followed me for miles telling me all about the other children that were working on the docks.

As I walked around the large market that was located adjacent to Elmina, I observed children working in various capacities. Many children were carrying loads of items on their heads, balancing heavy loads with perfect precision. They carried merchandise from one vendor to another. They delivered supplies, carried loads for consumers, and were paid very little for their efforts. Other children worked on the docks, salting fish for sale in the markets as the fish were unloaded from the fishing boats. This was a very tough and demanding job, I soon observed. One child told me about his life, working on the docks:

"I get up early in the morning and walk to the dock, where I help the people at the fish market prepare fish for sale. My job is to rub fish with salt when the next fishing boat comes in. Sometimes, I cut myself on the fish, and the salt makes my hands sting. For this, I receive my lunchtime meal, and a few Cedis. I stopped going to school last year, because I wasn't learning anything, and my family needs the money more than I needed to go to school."

## Selling Water

One of the most observable child labor activities I witnessed in Ghana was the "water girls." Young girls approximately 10-15 years of age carried large treys containing bagged water. This activity consisted mostly of selling bags of water to those who were visiting the Coast. They dominated the parking lots of all the slave castles, and were numerous around all the tourist zones. Most of them would work most of the day, did not attend school, and made very little money for their efforts.

Some of these children were actually selling water that they would retrieve from various sources, not all of which were potable. The girls were so mired in poverty that they would do almost anything for money. Scooping water out of a ditch, or a polluted stream was the least of their concerns. Selling it was a huge concern.

# Vending

Some children in Ghana sell items on the street, such as candy, trinkets of all sorts, and even common household items. These children are so visible on the streets of Accra that people routinely stop at the traffic lights to buy items from these children. Most of these children are working to help support their families. Others are street children which are trying to survive on their own.

# The Commercial Labor Market

The ILO estimates that about 20 percent of the people working in commercial agriculture in Africa are children. Some of them work part-time, and go to school. Commercial farming in Sub-Saharan Africa consists of a myriad of cash crops, such as manioc, coffee, tobacco, cocoa, tea, rice, fruits, sugar, groundnuts, rubber, and even cotton.

Some plantations employ numerous children to pick cotton and coffee. Job duties are grueling and labor intensive, but require little supervision, an ideal position for the employers. Such jobs would include weeding, picking, chopping sugar cane, cutting down cocoa fruits. These types of jobs require a good deal of bending and crawling. Typically, commercial farmers hire children because adults do not want such jobs. In such cases, children are paid lower, which increases the profits of the landowners and the bottom line of the companies.

# Working as Porters

One of the worst jobs children can perform is jobs as porters. Working as a porter is about as low as one can go in African society (Kielland & Tovo, 2004). Working as a porter means carrying heavy loads for other people. The loads are heavy, the fees are small, and the income is unreliable. It is considered a job of the last resort because it requires the ability to carry heavy items, requires endurance, strength, and a willingness to sweat.

In Ghana, the women and children who carry parcels in the markets go by the name *kayayei*. These are typically migrants from the countryside who work short-term to try and save money to start a small business. This is typical work for females who want to save up money for a dowry, as well.

These children are also seen in areas outside of busy areas, such as bus stations, airports, taxi stands, and other places where they can hustle people for a few Cedis. They are quite persistent, as well, and one quickly finds that they are handing over a few coins for some young boy or girl to carry suitcases or other bulky items.

## Cross Cultural Comparisons

It is essential to note that in most Western societies, children under the age of 18 are considered children, and are expected to attend school, not work. There are also laws that prohibit such employment of children, and especially the exploitation of child labor. However, that is not generally the case in most areas of Sub-Saharan Africa. One might make comparisons to Colonial America, where children were seen more as an economic asset. Or one might also compare this social problem to a time in America when children worked in factories for long hours at a time.

In general, then, most work by children in Sub-Saharan Africa is described as work that is duty bound by families. Most children are required to work around the house as a chore, and the cultural values of African families demand this of their children. So, in most cases, child labor, even though time-consuming and demanding, is a cultural phenomenon, and not considered harmful, even by the ILO. However, other forms of labor are considered cruel and exploitive, and are considered more harmful. These are known by the ILO as the "Worst Forms of Child Labor."

## The Worst Forms of Child Labor

Many forms of work performed by children have been labeled "worst forms," by the ILO, mainly because they jeopardize the health, safety, and morals of children. According to the ILO's Convention 182, Article 3, the worst forms of child labor are explained:

(a) All forms of slavery or practices similar to slavery, such as the sale and trafficking of children, debt bondage and serfdom and forced or compulsory labor, including forced or compulsory recruitment of children for use in armed conflict; (b) the use, procuring or offering of a child for prostitution, for the production of pornography or for pornographic performances; (c) the use, procuring or offering of a child for illicit activities, in particular for the production and trafficking of drugs as defined in the relevant international treaties; (d) work which, by its nature or the circumstances in which it is carried out, is likely to harm the health, safety or morals of children.

All of the children working in the worst forms of child labor have one thing in common: they are likely to be hurt to such an extent, that they may never recover to be normal citizens in their own communities. Two of these activities are described below.

## Quarrying and Mining

These two "worst forms" of child labor are essentially exploitative and hazardous. They prey on the children who are in the most desperate and poverty-stricken conditions. In 1996, the ILO estimated that 0.9 percent of economically active children worldwide worked in mines and quarries. In 2002, it estimated that at least 66 million children in Africa were economically active, and about 600,000 children are estimated to be working in these two industries.

Since gravel is in such a demand in most developing nations due to different types of construction, it is imperative that rocks in quarries be smashed to make small gravel. In most industrialized and developed countries, this type of work is handled by expensive machinery. In Africa, it is done by smashing large rocks with sledge hammers, thus breaking them into many smaller pieces. Of course, one way of keeping salaries down in these types of enterprises is to use children and pay them less.

There are quarries all over Africa, and are located near villages or cities that are populated by poor and destitute people. With this type of work comes long hours, hard manual labor, and is extremely dangerous work. Injuries are a constant part of the work, and breathing the dust of the constant breaking of the rocks causes a number of respiratory problems (Keilland & Tovo, 2004).

## Mining

Mining is another of the jobs that has been designated as harmful and dangerous. Africa has numerous natural resources, and mines are located in many places. There are gold mines, copper mines, iron, coal, nickel, as well as Uranium and even diamond mines scattered all over Sub-Saharan Africa.

Many of the mines in Africa resemble the Quarries, in the fact that the labor is tedious, difficult and dangerous. Boys tend to work in the mines, while girls work there bringing water to the workers. Many of the children that work in the mines become victims of child sexual abuse, or become child prostitutes. Unfortunately, this has become a major problem in Africa, and a very common one. Health officials in Burkina Faso, a country bordering Ghana, has reported a number of children with sexually transmitted diseases among the gold mining child populations that work in those mines (Kielland & Tovo, 2004).

## Consequences of Child Labor

While not all child labor is harmful in itself, there are some legitimate concerns about children who are working. Most of these effects are physiological, but, there are some psychological repercussions, as well.

## Physiological Effects

One of the many concerns is regarding the child's soft and not yet fully developed skeleton. Even the nervous system is still developing, and physicians, biologists, and physiotherapists have been examining some of the effects of hard labor on a child's body.

One of the chief requirements for a child that is working is the energy levels that may be required for the chosen task. If a child is not eating regularly, or is not getting enough of the proper nutrients, he may be harmed in the long run as far as physical health concerns (Kielland & Tovo, 2006).

Other concerns are that some of these jobs require heavy lifting, which may also harm the child if they are not properly developed. In the long run, some of these jobs may cause chronic pain, or disability. Other such concerns are the environmental hazards, as well as possible accidents and mishaps that may occur in the performance of their duties. This is especially true in mining, quarrying, and certain construction jobs.

In Sub-Saharan Africa, it is a given: children are going to work. It is a cultural phenomenon that has existed for centuries in Africa, and although Africa is changing, one thing that remains constant is that children are engaged in working. While some jobs are considered necessary for families and their economic conditions, others are more harmful and can cause permanent injury.

## The Supply and Demand Principle

As far as child labor demands go, it is essential to understand an underlying concept about such things as child labor. There is a profit to be made in child labor by unscrupulous owners, merchants, and employers. That is the demand. There is also a supply of children who must work. They are poor, vulnerable, and willing to put themselves in harm's way in order to survive. Therefore, the problem of child labor has persisted throughout the continent.

There are other forms of child labor that are considered harmful, as well. While mining and quarrying are harmful due to the heavy labor involved, and the risk of injury, there are other jobs much worse. One of these forms involves serving in the military. Child soldiering is one of the worst forms of child labor, and one of the most devastating. It has long term repercussions for children and the communities involved. Long term social and psychological problems also abound in this form of child labor.

# CHAPTER FIVE

# CHILD SOLDIERS IN SUB-SAHARAN AFRICA

## Child Soldiers

One of the worst forms of child labor in Africa is the problem of child soldiering. It seems odd that in the 21$^{st}$ Century, children should still be used in the performance of such things as war. It brings to mind haunting images of Adolph Hitler and his use of boy soldiers as he became more and more desperate in the final stages of World War II. However, one of the most egregious social problems of our time is still the "use of child soldiers."

## What is a Child Soldier?

The United Nations Children Fund (UNICEF) defines child soldiers as "any child—boy or girl—under eighteen years of age, who is part of any kind of regular or irregular armed force or armed group in any capacity." This age limit is relatively new, established in 2002 by the Optional Protocol to the Convention on the Rights of the Child (UNICEF, Children and Armed Conflict, 2003).

Prior to 2002, the 1949 Geneva Conventions and the 1977 Additional Protocols set "fifteen" as the minimum age for participation in armed conflict. While some debate exists over varying cultural standards of maturity, nearly 80 percent of conflicts involving child soldiers include combatants below the age of fifteen, with some as young as seven or eight.

## Cultural Variations

As Wessells, (2006), points out, in some areas in Africa, children are considered adults at various times in their lives, regardless of their age. For example, once a child experiences his or her initial rites of ceremony inducting them into adulthood, they are recognized as full-fledge adults, even though they may be under the age of 18. Culturally speaking, this remains a problem in some African societies, where age is not considered a factor.

## Prevalence

Today, there are still over 300,000 children engaged in combat on the planet. Most of these children are located on the continent of Africa, with numbers there, over 200,000. There are approximately another 50,000 in Latin America, and another 50,000 in Asia. Most experts will also agree that this number is probably a low estimate. This is because most militaries and governments do not admit to abducting children and soldiers, or recruiting children below the age of fifteen (Child Soldiers Global Report, 2008).

While the definition of childhood varies from culture to culture, the UN Convention on the Rights of the Child defines "child" broadly as "every human being below the age of 18 years." The 2007 *Paris Principles* interpret "a child associated with an armed force or armed group" as "any person below 18 years of age who is or who has been recruited or used by an armed force or armed group in any capacity, including but not limited to children, boys, and girls used as fighters, cooks, porters, messengers, spies or for sexual purposes." It does not only refer to a child who is taking or has taken a direct part in hostilities.

Most child soldiers are between the ages of 13 and 18, though many groups include children aged 12 and under. Ishmael Beah, a former child soldier who wrote the book, *Long Way Gone*, fought alongside a 7-year-old and an 11-year-old in Sierra Leone (Beah, 2008). The latter was mortally wounded by a rocket-propelled grenade. Beah recalls the incident with dread in his book, and as the small boy lay dying in front of him, Beah says "he cried for his mother in the most painfully piercing voice that I had ever heard."

Other scholars have found that in states such as Angola, Burundi, Congo, the Democratic Republic of Congo, Rwanda, Sudan and Uganda, children, some no more than seven or eight years of age, are recruited by government armed forces almost as a matter of course, while rebel forces in Sierra Leone were known to recruit children as young as five (Hanwanna, 2005).

In Uganda, children are caught in the battle between Uganda's People's Defense Force (UPDF) and the Lord's Resistance Army (LRA) rebel force, which is committed to overthrowing the Ugandan government and to this end rounds up children from villages it raids and forces them to join with them (Human Rights Watch, 1997). According to the report, one

16-year-old girl testified to the cruelties she endured when she witnessed a young boy who tried to escape:

> "One boy tried to escape, but he was caught. They made him eat a mouthful of red pepper, and five people were beating him. His hands were tied, and then they made us, the other new captives, kill him with a stick. I felt sick. I knew this boy from before. We were from the same village. I refused to kill him, and they told me they would shoot me. They pointed a gun at me, so I had to do it. The boy was asking me, "Why are you doing this?" I said I had no choice. After we killed him, they made us smear blood on our arms. I felt dizzy. They said we had to do this so we would not fear death, and so we would not try to escape."

Workers from the organization known as *Invisible Children* related to us in a visit to our campus in Texas recently, that the same fight that occurred in Uganda has now been moved to the Democratic Republic of the Congo, where they are still abducting children for the war. One young lady from Uganda told me that she hid in the jungle at night:

> "I hid in the jungle at night because we were afraid of being abducted in our own homes. We felt safer there. They took my cousin one night, and I haven't seen her since."

Most documented cases of child soldiering come from reports such as the "Child Soldiers Global Report," "Human Rights Watch," and other agencies at the United Nations. The evidence indicates that the majority of child soldiering occurs on the continent of Africa, but there are atrocities in Asia and Latin America, as well.

Violence has ravaged Burundi since the 1993 assassination of the country's first democratically elected president after a mere hundred days in office. More than half of Burundi's population is under eighteen, and the minimum legal age for military recruitment is sixteen. Yet, children as young as ten have played a significant role in the conflict, serving as combat troops, laborers, spies, and sex slaves for the Burundi armed forces as well as armed political groups. Although the major hostilities have ceased, sporadic fighting persists, and an estimated 5,000 child soldiers have yet to be demobilized (Child Soldiers Global Report, 2008).

The conflict that has ravaged the Democratic Republic of the Congo, (DRC), claiming an estimated 3 million lives since 1998, has seen some 30,000 children populate the ranks of government and rebel armies. Fifty percent of some opposition forces are children. Children serving in the *Congolese Rally* for *Democracy-Goma*, an armed political group, endure a particularly horrifying existence, experts say. The group's leader, Adolphe Onusumba, claims children join *RCD-Goma* voluntarily and benefit from the care and education they receive. In reality, analysts say most are abducted. Their "education" includes being forced to commit rape, killing their own relatives, and performing sexual or cannibalistic acts on the corpses of their enemies (Child Soldiers Global Report, 2008).

In Liberia, an August 2003 peace agreement put an end to the fourteen-year civil war that saw widespread use of child soldiers in both government and opposition forces. The national army even had a *Small Boys Unit* with commanders as young as twelve. "Most of these boys are orphans of the war," then-President Charles Taylor said.

> "Some of them saw their mothers wrapped in blankets, tied-up, and burned alive. We keep them armed as a means of keeping them out of trouble. It's a means of control."

When the conflict ended, an estimated 21,000 children needed to be reintegrated into Liberian society. In November 2005, little violence was reported in Liberia's first presidential elections since the war, though many observers worried that former child veterans would revolt when the candidate they favored, George Weah, was defeated (Child Soldiers Global Report, 2008).

The long war in Sierra Leone was a direct result of Charles Taylor's incursion into the country, using child soldiers against the citizens of Sierra Leone. Sierra Leone had their own young children participate in the war against Liberia and the *RUF*, or the *Revolutionary United Front*. This horrific account of child soldiering is brought to light in Ishmael Beah's account in his autobiography previously mentioned (Beah, 2008). This bloody war, using child soldiers was also documented in the popular movie, "Blood Diamond."

# The Guilty Countries

## Uganda

Children serve in the ranks of the government's *Uganda Peoples' Defense Force* as well as in the opposing *Lord's Resistance Army* (LRA). According to Brookings Institute Senior Fellow Peter W. Singer, the LRA is "effectively a cult with a core of just 200 adult members," who has been able to prolong the conflict by abducting some 25,000 children and forcing them into their ranks. LRA units carry out widespread attacks on civilians, killing, raping, and looting. Kidnappings are so widespread that Amnesty

International reported in November 2005 an estimated 30,000 "night commuters"—children hoping to avoid abduction—were seeking refuge in urban areas each night.

## Sudan

According to some sources, the numerous armed forces and groups that are parties to the conflict in the Sudan has a long history of using children for military purposes. One report states that there are five armed groups recruiting the use of children for purposes of war: The *Janjaweed,* the *JEM,* the *SSUM,* the *SLA,* and the *SPLA (*Children and Armed Conflict in Sudan, 2009).

Much of the violence in Sudan, which has created over 1 million refugees, has been attributed to militias known as the *Janjaweed.* The word, an Arabic colloquialism, means "a man with a gun on a horse." *Janjaweed* militiamen are primarily members of nomadic Arab tribes who've long been at odds with Darfur's settled African farmers, who are darker-skinned. Until 2003, the conflicts were mostly over Darfur's scarce water and land resources—desertification has been a serious problem, so grazing areas and wells are at a premium. In fact, the term "*Janjaweed*" has for years been synonymous with bandit, as these horse-or-camel-borne fighters were known to swoop in on non-Arab farms to steal cattle.

The *Janjaweed* started to become much more aggressive in 2003, after two non-Arab groups, the *Sudan Liberation Army* and the *Justice and Equality Movement* took up arms against the Sudanese government, alleging mistreatment by the Arab regime in Khartoum. In response to the uprising, the *Janjaweed* militias began pillaging towns and villages inhabited by members of the African tribes from which the rebel armies draw their strength—the *Zaghawa, Masalit*, and *Fur* tribes. (This conflict is entirely separate from the 22-year-old civil war that has pitted the Muslim government against Christian and animist rebels in the country's southern region. The *Janjaweed*, who inhabit western Sudan, have nothing to do with that war.)

In March 2004, there were an estimated 17,000 children in government forces allied militias and opposition armed groups in the north, east and south. Between 2,500 and 5,000 children served in the armed opposition group, the *Sudan's People's Liberation Army* (SPLA), in the south. Despite a widely publicized child demobilization program, in which it claimed to have demobilized over 16,000 children between 2001 and 2004, the SPLA continued to recruit and train child soldiers. In 2003 it was reported that armed groups were active in government armed forces,

Janjaweed militias, and opposition groups (Children and Armed Conflict in Sudan, 2009).

## Why use Child Soldiers?

Both governments and armed groups use children because they are easier to condition into fearless killing and unthinking obedience. Children are a cheap and plentiful resource for military commanders in need of a steady troop supply to war zones. Their underdeveloped ability to assess danger means they are often willing to take risks and difficult assignments that adults or older teenagers will refuse. Children are more impressionable than adults, and depending on their age and background, their value systems and consciences are not yet fully developed (Amnesty International, 2005).

In the case of Ishmael Beah, he refers to the drug use of mixing gunpowder and cocaine as well as giving the children marijuana (Beah, 2008). Military commanders have been known to use proven tactics to produce unquestioning obedience in these homesick children while transforming them into killers. New recruits are often forced to kill or perpetrate various acts of violence against others, including strangers, escapees or even members of their own village or family. Coercing the children to harm or kill people they know has the added benefit of discouraging them from attempting escape, as they know they will no longer be welcome back home.

Some groups also practice cannibalism, making young recruits drink the blood or eat the flesh of their victims, attempting to convince them that it will make them stronger. One expert on child soldiering, Michael Wessells, (2006) argues that the real motivation is to force children to quiet their emotional reactions to seeing people killed and demolish their sense of the sanctity of life and their tendency to show respect for the dead (Wessells, 2006). Revenge is also used as a motivator. Ishmael Beah's commanders told him to "visualize the enemy, the rebels who killed your parents, your family, and those who are responsible for everything that has happened to you."

## How are Child Soldiers Recruited?

A U.N. study was led by children's rights activist Graca Machel, the former first lady of Mozambique, and it was learned that children usually become soldiers through coercion, either through mandatory conscription or forced recruitment (UNICEF, "The Machel Study," 1996).

When national armies have a manpower shortfall, they may find it convenient not to search too carefully for the accurate birth date of a conscript. Rebel forces seldom have use for birth records, either. In countries covered by the case studies, government forces as well as rebel forces were often equally likely to use child soldiers.

## Recruitment by Abduction

In Ethiopia, armed militias would surround a public area such as a marketplace, order every male to sit down, and then force into a truck anyone deemed "eligible." At particular risk of abduction were teenagers who worked on the streets selling cigarettes or candy. Forced abductions, says the Machel Study, were commonly one element in a larger campaign to intimidate communities. Armed groups that abduct children for soldiering are also inclined to go on rape-and-looting rampages while in the villages.

Militias often use brutish methods to weaken resistance to forcible recruitment. The case study for Uganda reports that people who resisted attacks by the *Lord's Resistance Army* would be cut with pangas (machetes). Quite a number of victims had their lips and ears chopped off in macabre rituals. To seal off possible avenues of resistance from the children's communities, recruiters may deliberately destroy the bonds of trust between child and community. In Mozambique, for instance, recruiters from RENAMO forced boy recruits to kill someone from their own village.

Governments in a few countries legally conscript children under 18, but even where the legal minimum age is18, the law is not necessarily a safeguard. In many countries, birth registration is inadequate or non-existent and children do not know how old they are. Recruiters can only guess at ages based on physical development and may enter the age of recruits as 18 to give the appearance of compliance with national laws.

According to the Machel Report, countries that have weak administrations, (such as most developing nations), recruits are arbitrarily seized on the streets, or from schools or orphanages. Children from poorer sectors of society are particularly vulnerable. Adolescent boys, who work in the informal sector selling cigarettes or gum or lottery tickets, are a particular target. Orphanages, street children, working children all provide the "supply" for military use.

## Economic Reasons

Just as we have already stated, economics can be a major issue, as well. As the Machel study points out, hunger and poverty may drive parents to offer their children for service. In some cases, armies pay a minor soldier's wages directly to the family. Child participation may also be difficult to distinguish as in some cases whole families move with armed groups. Children themselves may volunteer if they believe that this is the only way to guarantee regular meals, clothing or medical attention. Some case studies tell of parents who encourage their daughters to become soldiers if their marriage prospects are poor.

Some children also feel obliged to become soldiers for their own protection. Faced with violence and chaos all around, they decide they are safer with guns in their hands. In some societies, military life may be the most attractive option. Young people often take up arms to gain power, and power can act as a very strong motivator in situations where people feel powerless and are otherwise unable to acquire basic resources.

In many situations, war activities are glorified. In Sierra Leone, Wessells, (2006), met with child soldiers who proudly defended the number of "enemies" they had killed. The lure of ideology is particularly strong in early adolescence, when young people are developing personal identities and searching for a sense of social meaning.

## Recruiting Girls

Although the majority of child soldiers are boys, armed groups also recruit girls, many of whom perform the same functions as boys. Some rebel groups use girls to prepare food, attend to the wounded and wash clothes. Girls may also be forced to provide sexual services. In Uganda, girls who are abducted by the Lord's Resistance Army are "married off" to rebel leaders. If the man dies, the girl is put aside for ritual cleansing and then married off to another rebel.

## Child Soldiering in Ghana

In 2005 the government reported to the UN Committee on the Rights of the Child that the minimum age for voluntary enlistment into the army was 18, that there was no conscription and that by law under-18s were not allowed to join the armed forces. There were no reports of under-18 children in the armed forces. However, refugees had entered the country in several stages as a result of the Sierra Leone war and Liberian incursions, as well as refugees from Togo that had fled to Ghana to escape government violence. Ghana has also led in the battle against using child soldiers in Africa.

## Post-Traumatic Stress and Long Term Effects of Child Soldiering

There are many long term effects of child soldiering. Some of the most obvious results are that they are separated from their parents and lose their homes. They are exposed to violence, death, and are often permanently disabled. Physical injury also carries additional emotional, psychological, and social disadvantages. Yet the most severe long term consequences of children serving as soldiers may be their moral development. When the fighting ends it's very hard to place these kids back in a home surrounding, or school surrounding and expect them to adjust. They are in fear all of the time, and have a difficult time switching over from a non-violent life style if they are even to adjust at all. Studies have been conducted on the repercussions of child soldiers from the *Revolutionary United Front* and their eventual return to society (Denov, M. 2010).

## Rejection and Stigmatization

Once the conflict in Sierra Leone was over, the majority of boys and girls formerly with the *RUF* reported experiencing some form of rejection and/or stigmatization by their families and the community as a result of their former affiliation with the *RUF*. These experiences were described as particularly painful and debilitating. Many children were branded on their bodies by rebel forces with the letters 'RUF' or 'AFRC'. These children continue to suffer shame, stigma and rejection as a result.

The stigma associated with former girl soldiers appears to be particularly problematic. Girls were alienated because of their affiliation with the rebels, and also because many of them had been victims of sexual violence. Within the context of Africa as elsewhere, women and girls who experience sexual violence are often later ostracized by their families and communities, due to becoming "unmarriageable," because of the rape and sexual acts committed toward them. This was especially true given the importance of virginity in a marriage in Africa (Denov, 2010).

# Unwanted Pregnancy

Importantly, it is not only the individual rape victim who may be stigmatized. A few girls reported that their children borne of rape were rejected or vilified by their broader family and community. Given the complex circumstances, girls also reported experiencing conflicting feelings towards their children. Some girls reported taking out their frustrations on their children by beating them.

# Physical Consequences

While amidst the armed groups, the vast majority of participants reported having experienced some form of serious injury. Many children reported being left disabled and were living with the pain and discomfort of their injuries. This was especially true for those girls who had been subjected to rape and violence, and often reported gynecological problems, as well. Although the children suffered physical injuries, oftentimes, the psychological scars were more significant than the pain of physical injury, and all the injuries, both psychological and physical were torturous reminders of what they had endured.

# Guilt and Shame

Most of the children who had engaged in combat suffered from guilt and shame over what they had done as child soldiers. Some of them retained haunting images of the violence they had committed, while remembering traumatic incidents they had witnessed firsthand.

# Displacement and Sense of Loss

While almost all of the child soldiers in the Denov study reported being displaced from their homes and families, as well as their communities, they suffered a significant sense of loss, separation, depression, and anxiety as a result. Some children reported that they had not been able to locate members of their families, and had no place to go, or anyone to take care of them once the conflict was over (Denov, 2010).

# Reintegration of Child Soldiers

According to scholars working on the Denov research project, (2010), with these children, reintegration was something that became extremely important. Among the many needs of children who were soldiers included the following:

- Clinical and cultural treatment for post-traumatic stress
- Cultural and clinical counseling and therapy
- Prevention, management and treatment of diseases, including HIV/AIDS
- Peer socialization
- Empowerment and restoration of girls stigmatized by sexual abuse and rape
- Literacy, education and skills training
- Arts, culture, sports and recreation activities
- Jobs creation and job-readiness skills
- Reproductive health counseling and training
- Diversion from criminal justice systems
- Drug and alcohol rehabilitation
- Participation with projects that build peace and a culture of human and children's rights
- Reintegration into family and community

In some cases, because some child soldiers killed family members, or those in the community that they knew, they are not able to return home to their communities. Sometimes, third party organizations must help to facilitate the former child soldier's return to his family and community, and help the family and community to prepare in advance.

Child soldiering is one of the most reprehensible acts of the globalized community. Children that have engaged in combat have been found to suffer from short and long term psychological and emotional difficulties, as outlined above by the Denov studies. Post-Traumatic Stress alone runs rampant through the populations of children that have been forced to fight wars they did not understand.

Not only is child soldiering a reprehensible act, it is almost an unknown fact among most average citizens that live in first world countries. As a college professor, I assign Ishmael Beah's book, *Long Way Gone*, to my classes. I am always amazed at how few students are aware of the problem in general. A lot of people are aware of the bloody war that raged in Sierra Leone and the RUF because of the popular movie, "Blood Diamond," but are not familiar with the travesty of the child soldiers that were involved in that war.

So, in the realm of child labor, there are many social problems that abound in Sub-Saharan Africa. Whether it be working in the household, or working in the mines and quarries of Africa, children are working. Sometimes they are used for cheap, exploitable labor, and are exploited into forms known as the "Worst Forms of Child Labor." Sometimes, it is a cultural phenomenon that is undertaken more for survival than for exploitation. Even the more reprehensible acts, such as child soldiering can be a form of survival for many, as their chances of receiving an education is minimal. Their economic future is in doubt, and being in the military offers them more of a life than anything else they can turn to.

Another population that arises in the category of child labor is street children, who in the transition of moving from rural communities to the modern day urbanization have increased in numbers due to the changing nature of families in Africa. These children work various areas, and may develop unique lifestyles that become another area of concern in Ghana and Sub-Saharan Africa.

# CHAPTER SIX

# THE SOCIAL PROBLEMS OF STREET CHILDREN

## A Worldwide Phenomenon

### Prevalence

One of the most alarming social problems of children on this planet is the large numbers of "street children." Currently, UNICEF estimates the numbers at between 150-170 million worldwide. I spent the first few years of my academic career researching and observing street children in Latin America, Africa, and Asia, and the problems they face are almost insurmountable.

I began my research on street children in 2003, while living in Latin America, most notably Mexico and Peru. It was from that research that drew me to Africa to make some comparisons and observe conditions in Africa. Street children seem to form their own culture, and learn a number of survival techniques that help them to adapt to the streets in Latin America, as well as Africa.

The numbers of street children vary from region to region, but the breakdown according to UNICEF for Africa is approximately 30-50 million, while Latin America is hovering around 50 million, and Asia has approximately another 25-30 million, with India accounting for about 11-15 million of those numbers in Asia (UNICEF, 2005).

In some countries, street children are shot down like vermin to rid the streets of them. In other places, they are kidnapped, sold into prostitution, or sexually and physically abused. Most populations of street children, (90 percent) become addicted to drugs within the first year they are on the streets (Hollingsworth, 2008). Because some of them are homeless, they become vulnerable populations. Yet, not all street children are homeless. There are actually several categories of street children, each of which may form a different lifestyle and culture. While UNICEF becomes one of the most important agencies dealing with street children, they offer some definitions that are worth exploring.

# Definitions of Street Children

## Market Children

For the purposes of this book, the term "Street children" will be used to describe at least three separate categories of children that make up this subculture. First, there are those known as *market children*, who work in the streets selling and begging for their survival, but returning home to their families at night. Market children are helping to provide another source of income for their families. A large majority of the street children in Sub-Saharan Africa are market children, just as they are in Latin America.

In Ghana, the migration of children to urban areas and cities has swelled the numbers of children living and surviving in the streets. Eric Beauchemin, (1999), in "The Exodus," documents the frustrations in some of the lives of street children living in Ghana as they migrated to the cities:

> "My five brothers and sisters have never been to school. I dropped out of primary because my parents couldn't afford the school fees. I'm not doing anything at the moment, but I want to become a seamstress. I'd like to do my apprenticeship in Takoradi, because it's not too far away. I'm hoping that my parents will give me money to go. I don't know how much I need, but 20,000 Cedis (About $9 at that time) should be enough. It doesn't matter if I have to sleep on the street. Anything is better than staying here. There's no future here."

The child in Beauchemin's report can be typically described as a market child. He has an intact family, but is practically on his own, living hand to mouth, trying to survive and help out his family. I had the opportunity to talk to many children like that while working in Ghana. Most of the children I encountered on the streets were market children. They talked fondly of their parents, but one young male who was trying to pickpocket me told me the following story:

> "My father is working away in the city, and my mother is all alone, trying to raise my brothers and sisters. I work because my mother cannot afford to feed us. So, I walked to Accra to find a job as a fisherman. I worked for this one guy, but he would not pay me. I worked for food, and that is all. I am now trying to find work, but it is hard. Life is hard."

The interesting thing about this young boy is that we talked for a long time outside the city of Accra, and he kept reaching in my pocket to jingle the change I had. He was a rather poor pick-pocket, but he did win my sympathy, and I gave him the change I had. I met many of the same market children, working as porters, selling water to tourists, or working on the docks, salting fish in Cape Coast.

Cape Coast, since it had so many tourists, was a popular place for children to find work. They would try and find work as guides, or taking pictures of tourists. Most people treated them with a great deal of indifference as they mostly found the boys and girls to be pests. These market children sacrifice a good portion of their lives, including their education, to work and help support their families.

Many of the market children I interviewed were more than glad to tell me about their lives. They counted on tourists around popular areas, but did not restrict their sales tactics toward them. For one thing, Accra is not the tourist capital of the world by any means. While the market children in Accra would stand on street corners, selling homemade jewelry, the children on the Cape Coast area would be selling water or trying to serve as guides for tourists in the slave castles. One child told me:

> "I always try and sell something to people from America, because they are all rich. Sometimes they just walk away and won't even look at me, though."

## Comparison with Latin America

Latin American market street children, ranging in age from four to 18, have parents who cannot afford to send them to school. So they work on the streets for income--washing car windows, shining shoes, and selling food. At night, these children go home to their families. Those with families and homes represent about 60 percent of Latin America's estimated 40-50 million street children.

Working with street children in Mexico and Peru, I quickly observed an interesting phenomenon about street children in general, but especially with market children, and that was what I refer to as "pseudo adulthood." These children, regardless of their age were fast becoming "little adults." They drank alcohol, they smoked cigarettes, and they cursed regularly, worse than most adults I ever knew. They also had fewer social skills outside of what they actually learned on the streets to sell their products, or to make money. The social skills they would have developed by playing games or going to school with peers was almost absent.

## Pseudo-Adulthood in Ghana

In direct comparison to the children in Latin America, the market children in Ghana and Sub-Saharan Africa retained a lot of the same cultural traits. These children did not think like children, or play like children. Most of the market children in Ghana became adults at early ages, as did the market children in Mexico and Peru. There was very little "play-time" for the children in Ghana, as they were too busy trying to find work to support their families, as did the market children in Latin America.

## Lack of School Attendance

Market children in Ghana also shared the same school attendance trait as the children in Mexico and Peru. Their education was sacrificed in order to work, although, some did attend school in Ghana on a part time basis. One interesting statement I heard over and over from children in Ghana, was that "work" was more important than "school." In several cases, it has been stated that because of the conditions of the schools in Ghana and other countries in Sub-Saharan Africa, children were better off working than attending school.

## Homeless Children

Another form of street children, are the *homeless street children*, who work, live, and sleep in the streets, often lacking any contact with their families, or have been totally abandoned. Some of these children have run away from their homes because of abuse or violence, and have had to live in the streets on a permanent basis. These children range from 6 to 18 years of age. Homeless street children may work, beg, or pickpocket to finance their lifestyles. I encountered several who tried to beg outright for money.

Homeless street children often get the most attention, because they can be easily manipulated, exploited, and preyed upon by shameless sexual traffickers, or policemen who receive extra pay for ridding the population of homeless urchins who are just seen as a problem to be "cleaned up." Homeless children may live in sewers, abandoned buildings, or in cardboard boxes. They often are the ones most susceptible to drug use, as well. They may be orphans released from orphanages at the age of 12 or 13, and become a major part of the "supply" side of child traffickers and exploiters of children for labor opportunities.

# Increasing Numbers

In Ghana, we are seeing many more homeless children living in the streets due to the large numbers of children leaving rural areas and migrating to cities like Accra, and Kumasi, the two largest cities in Ghana. Other problems are exacerbating the situation, as well, such as the AIDS pandemic.

In Ghana, it has been reported that there are over 70,000 children who are out of school, living on the streets in Accra, the capital city. They are poor, and survive any way they can, including acting as porters, selling water, or vending products on street corners. Others may steal for their survival, or pickpocket strangers for small change. Other sources have a different story on the numbers. Ghana's Department of Social Welfare and local NGO's believe that there are about 21,000 children living and working on Accra's streets, with no parents to protect them. They also report that there could be as many as another 50,000 living in Kumasi, Ghana's second largest city.

Several children I interviewed showed me where they were living. One child showed me a cardboard box that he had been living in. Inside, he showed me pictures of his sisters that he had drawn on the inside. He had also colored in a picture of his mother, whom he had not seen in several years. He was approximately ten years of age, and he was an excellent guide. He took me around the market area explaining everything about the area. He related this story to me:

> "I started off working on the streets when I was seven because my father told me to leave. My mother had AIDS and was not doing well. My father would beat me every night, so one day, I did leave. I was selling bracelets that I got from a man who owned a street vending business. I am now ten, and I have been living on the streets for three years. One day, I plan to own my own store."

The young boy was an expert on the history of El Mina and the Atlantic Slave Trade. He knew the area very well, and he showed me one area where the ships would come in near the dock. We walked around the fish market, where he showed me several other boys who were working as vendors and porters. One boy was carrying a load of salted fish for a customer. He was moving very fast with his load perched on his head, balanced perfectly.

## Comparisons with Latin America

In Mexico, while researching and observing homeless street children, I learned that children often huddle together at night, using drugs or huffing products to make them high, and then further "escape" by having sex as early as 10 years of age. Many of the girls I interviewed would have sex at night with boys and then would fall asleep. I always viewed this as another coping mechanism that they adopted to make up for the loneliness and the lack of love and attention, (Hollingsworth, 2008).

In Africa, obviously, the homeless children live together in the same fashion, living wherever they can to protect them from the elements. I saw children living in cardboard boxes, sewers, under bridges, and down on the beach where they would "hang out" in large numbers. My assessment of homeless children in Ghana was that there was a problem of migration and early release of orphans from institutions, or from having parents that were dying of AIDS that created a large percentage of the street children.

## Street Family Children

Lastly, there are those children defined as *street family children*, who live on the streets alongside their families, and beg for their survival. These children are from poverty-stricken families, and range anywhere from 3-17 years of age. Sub-Saharan Africa is seeing an increase in these families, as poverty has become so widespread in the region. However, in comparison with Mexico and Latin America, the numbers are quite different. In Sub-Saharan Africa, it seems that most of the families die younger and therefore don't survive the streets very well, thus leaving more children homeless.

## Comparisons with Latin America

Large numbers of children in Mexico live on the streets alongside their families, and beg for their survival. These children are from poverty-stricken families, and range anywhere from 3-17 years of age. If you were in Mexico City at any given time, you would run across this situation almost instantly as you walked down the street. You would see a mother, with dirty hair, no shoes, sitting against a wall while her children danced or sang for the passers-by. She might have a tin cup for you to throw money into, or the children may be playing a musical instrument. Even worse, the children may just chase you down with their hands out, begging for money.

This situation is not seen as much in Ghana, as families are one of the strongest units in their culture. If the families are intact, they are generally not seen living and begging together on the streets. The extended family, if it still exists, is the first line of defense.

## Drug Use among Street Children

### Comparisons with Latin America

In Peru, after many observations and interviews with street children in Lima and in Cusco, it became evident that there was a major use of inhalants, as it was throughout Latin America among the homeless children populations. Since Peru is one of the chief Coca Leaf producing countries in South America, the children were smoking a product called "basuco." Basuco was a jungle-refined coca paste product that produced hallucinations and became highly psychologically addictive.

One study by an organization that serves street children in four Latin American countries, reports that over 90 percent of the street children in Mexico sniff glue or other inhalants (Casa Alianza Study, 2000). One of the main products that is huffed by children in Mexico is a paint thinner product called *Dismex*. Others use shoe glue produced by a company in Minnesota, called H.B. Fuller.

Over the years, H.B. Fuller has received a large amount of criticism in the press for manufacturing a product they know has been abused by street children in Latin America. Some critics have called for the manufacturer to make products without the toxic substance Toluene, or to add ingredients that would make the children vomit after "huffing" these products. This controversy still looms, and public comments from the Fuller company are practiced and avoidant according to most Latin American authorities (Hollingsworth, 2008).

While observing homeless street children in Mexico, I was able to observe firsthand the inhalant abuse inside an abandoned building where children would gather and inhale Dismex. They would sit in a circle, spray the product onto the sleeves of their shirts and inhale deeply. Eventually, their eyes would become glassy, and before long they would drift off to sleep. I observed this phenomenon in several populations of street children in Mexico.

# Problems in Sub-Saharan Africa

In Latin America, where two-fifths of the earth's 150 million street children live, inhalant abuse, particularly glue-sniffing, is pandemic. It is also a problem around the globe. A Kenyan group that rehabilitates street children estimates that 52-90 percent of Kenyan street children are addicted to their glue inhalation habit. According to a government estimate, there are 50,000 street children in Nairobi and 300,000 living around the country; the number of children addicted to glue has the potential to be astronomically high. Glue is a drug of choice; cheap and easy to get, it quells hunger pangs and keeps the cold at bay (NACADA, 2004).

While the use of inhalants is a common problem in Sub-Saharan Africa as it is in Latin America, there is a growing tendency to use less commonly known drugs. I was quite astounded to find the use of Jenkem and Khat in use in some populations of street children in Sub-Saharan Africa.

## The Use of Jenkem

In Ghana, I discovered a small group of children who were actually sniffing "sewer gas," which was mostly fermented human waste products taken from a cesspool and kept in a jar for sniffing. The concoction caused massive hallucinations, which produced visions of some of their dead ancestors. This product is known as *Jenkem.*

Others have also reported on this phenomenon in Zambia during the 1990's (Guest, 2001). It is described as fermented human sewage scraped from pipes and stored in plastic bags for a week or so. The fumes are numbing and intoxicating.

## The Use of Khat

Khat is another product used by street children in Africa. It is a stimulant with much of the same quality as methamphetamine effects. The khat plant is known by a variety of names, such as *qat* and *gat* in Yemen, *qaat* and *jaad* in Somalia, and *chat* in Ethiopia. It is also known as *jimma* in the Oromo language and *miraa* in the Meru Language. Khat has been grown for use as a stimulant for centuries in the Horn of Africa and the Arabian Peninsula. Within the counter-culture segments of the Kenyan elite population, khat is used to counter the effects of a hangover or binge drinking, similar to the use of the coca leaf in South America. Khat is typically chewed like tobacco. The fresh leaves, twigs, and shoots of the khat shrub are chewed, and then retained in the cheek and chewed intermittently to release the active drug. Dried plant material can be made into tea or a chewable paste, but dried khat is not as potent as the fresh plant product. Khat can also be smoked and even sprinkled on food. Compulsive use may result in manic behavior with grandiose delusions or in a paranoid type of illness, sometimes accompanied by hallucinations.

Street children typically chew the plant for the same reason that street children in Latin America sniff glue, to tame the effects of hunger, and counteract the loneliness from living on the streets. Other methods of drugs in street children are inhaling through a wet carbon paper, inhaling vapor produced by a mixture of fiber matting and boiling toothpaste, inhaling fumes from burning insects, and inhalation of raw sewage (World Health Report, 1994).

## The Dangers of Inhalant Abuse

The consequences of Inhalant abuse result in a vast array of devastating medical consequences. Prolonged sniffing of the highly concentrated chemicals in solvents or aerosol sprays can induce irregular and rapid heart rhythms and can lead to heart failure and death within minutes of a session of prolonged sniffing. In addition, many organs of the body are adversely affected by the chemical Toluene, which is contained within several of the products street children use for huffing.

Toluene is a clear, colorless liquid with a distinctive smell. Toluene occurs naturally in crude oil and in the Tolu tree. It is also produced in the process of making gasoline and other fuels from crude oil and making coke from coal. Toluene is used in making paints, paint thinners, fingernail polish, lacquers, adhesives, and rubber and in some printing and leather tanning processes.

The euphoria experienced by huffing glue, for example, is the result of toluene's toxic effects on the brain. Just as it effectively dissolves plastics, it also dissolves brain cells and other organ tissue. Reacting to this damage, the brain becomes flooded with soothing endorphins and, for a brief time, children actually feel no hunger, no cold, and no discomfort. When the period passes, they experience desperation and crave more glue for relief, thus developing a full-blown psychic addiction.

Inhaling High levels of toluene in a short time can make an individual feel light-headed, dizzy, or sleepy. It can also cause unconsciousness, and even death. Breathing large amounts of toluene for short periods of time adversely affects the human nervous system, the kidneys, the liver, and the heart. Effects range from unsteadiness and tingling in fingers and toes to unconsciousness and death. Direct, prolonged contact with toluene liquid or vapor irritates the skin and the eyes.

Human health effects associated with breathing or otherwise consuming smaller amounts of toluene over long periods of time are not precisely known. However, repeatedly breathing large amounts of toluene, such as when huffing glue or paint, can cause permanent brain damage. As a result, humans can develop problems with speech, hearing, and vision. Humans can also experience loss of muscle control, loss of memory, and decreased mental ability. Exposure to toluene can also adversely affect the kidneys.

## What Causes the Street Children Problem?

The AIDS epidemic and civil wars in Africa have caused a surge in the number of street children as a result of the abandonment of AIDS orphans or fatalities due to armed conflict. Failing economies and falling currencies in parts of Asia force the poorest families onto the street, often leaving children abandoned and homeless. Children often experience the effects of political, economic, and social crises within their countries more severely than adults, and many lack the adequate institutional support to address their special needs. Eventually, they end up on the streets (Kopoka, 2000).

Children who are vulnerable to street life include those who have been abandoned by their families or sent into cities because of a family's intense poverty, often with hopes that a child will be able to earn money for the family and send it home. Children who run away from home or children's institutions frequently end up on the street since they rarely return home due to dysfunctional families, or physical, mental, and/or sexual abuse. In several areas of the world, disabled children are commonly abandoned, particularly in developing countries. In addition, refugee children of armed conflict areas, children separated from their families for long periods of time, and AIDS orphans, repeatedly find nowhere to go but the streets.

One major problem that leads to homelessness is that some orphanages release their children at young ages as their numbers in the facilities climb. In Ghana, most orphanages were letting their children leave at early as 13 years of age. Without an education, job skills, or family involvement, most of these children will end up on the streets. This was my observation upon the conclusion of my field work in Africa inside the orphanages.

## The Effects of Street and Homeless Life

Homelessness and street life have extremely detrimental effects on children (Family Housing Fund Report, 1999). Their unstable lifestyles, lack of medical care, and inadequate living conditions increase young people's susceptibility to chronic illnesses such as respiratory or ear infections, gastrointestinal disorders, and sexually-transmitted diseases, including HIV/AIDS. Children living on their own must find ways to eat; some scavenge or find exploitative physical work. Many homeless children are enticed by adults and older youth into selling drugs, stealing, and prostitution. Drug use by children on the streets is common as they look for means to numb the pain and deal with the hardships associated with street life. Studies have found that up to 90 percent of street children use psychoactive substances, including medicines, alcohol, cigarettes, heroin, cannabis, and readily available industrial products such as shoe glue. So, whether its Latin American street children sniffing Dismex, or shoe glue, or Peruvian children sniffing Basuco, a form of coca paste made from coca leaves, the effects are the same. Children are numbing themselves to their circumstances. The mental, social and emotional growth of children are also affected by their nomadic lifestyles and the way in which they are chastised by authorities who constantly expel them from their temporary homes such as doorways, park benches, and railway platforms.

## Long Range Problems of Street Children

Street children generally lack the basic resources for a healthy lifestyle. They wear dirty clothes or not enough clothes in the winter time. They may go hungry for long stretches of time. When I was observing this condition in Mexico, I had street children come into the restaurants where I was eating and try to eat off of my plate.

Street children may also lack safe drinking water, or have less accessibility to sanitation and toilets, which may lead to health problems. In Africa, I learned that children were getting hookworms and other parasites from drinking dirty water. The most significant risk of hookworm infection is anemia, secondary to loss of iron (and protein) in the gut. Other health problems of street children are also quite apparent, such as diseases they may obtain due to lack of adequate immunization and vaccinations.

The lack of education is also one of the worst problems street children face. In Sub-Saharan Africa, very few of the children were going to school.   This condemns them to a working life for the rest of their immediate future.   Without an education, they would never receive adequate skills to improve their lives or the lives of their future children. Homeless children are more likely to score poorly on math, reading, spelling, and vocabulary tests if they are lucky enough to attend school (Family Housing Fund Report, P. 3.).

## Safety Concerns

The streets in developing countries are not entirely safe, so street children face eminent danger from a variety of sources.   They may be targeted by police, gangs, drug syndicates, those who operate commercial sex businesses, death squads and a host of other dangerous activities. Being a street child also makes one vulnerable for many child labor and exploitative individuals looking for cheap labor, or for those who may be recruiting child soldiers.

## Long Range Psychological Problems

Many of the situations that eventually caused these children to flee to the streets may have long-term implications for their mental health.  The severe implications of physical, sexual, or mental abuse that caused children to leave their families in the first place will have major repercussions for their mental health.  For example, they may have identity problems, abandonment issues, depression or anxiety, post-traumatic stress, or developmental problems that will haunt them for many years (Family Housing Fund Report, P. 3).

Street children may also suffer from social isolation and extreme loneliness, as well as difficulties in developing relationships.   Lack of social skills they would have gotten had they been afforded an education, as well as a lack of employable or marketing job skills will follow them the rest of their lives, with negative implications for their futures.   Of course, there are the long term effects of the use of psychoactive drugs, pregnancy from unprotected sex, diseases such as HIV/AIDS or other sexually transmitted diseases.

Street children live and work amidst trash, animals and open sewers. Not only are they exposed and susceptible to disease, they are also unlikely to be vaccinated or receive medical treatment. Very few African children have been vaccinated against TB, Diphtheria, Tetanus, Polio and Measles; only one in ten against Hepatitis B. Most street children have not been vaccinated at all.

Street children may be a problem for many years to come. Currently, as long as crowded urban centers exist, and as long as abusive parents exist, and as long as war, conflict, AIDS, and poverty exist, the problem of street children promises to continue. In developing nations, where poverty is highest, and AIDS has become such a significant impact, it seems unlikely that the problem with street children will lessen any time soon. In the meantime, street children continue to be involved in such things as drug use and larceny. Some street children begin criminal careers after realizing that their chances of having a better life are next to impossible.

## Human Needs for Survival and Maslow's Hierarchy of Needs

In Sub-Saharan Africa, as well as in Latin America, street children often join gangs for protection, as well as for a sense of belonging. Abraham Maslow first spoke to this part of human development when he formed the theory of the *Hierarchy of Needs* in 1954. In a sense, Maslow explains that all humans have certain requirements for survival, or what he terms "self-actualization," and he outlined these in the form of a pyramid. He begins by placing "physiological needs" at the bottom of the pyramid. They are obviously those basic needs required for human survival, such as food, clothing and shelter. If these needs are not met, humans cannot self-actualize. Self-actualization refers here to mean "meeting one's own potential in life."

Street children, especially homeless street children are lacking in these physiological needs. Food is a luxury, proper clothing is not adequate, and shelter to keep out of the elements is not present, creating a demand for survival that may be out of reach for most homeless street kids.

The next item on Maslow's list is "safety needs." In order for a person to be well-developed, they need personal safety in the form of personal security, financial security, health and well-being, and safety against illness. Street children suffer drawbacks from each of these concerns. They are not secure on the streets. They are an extremely vulnerable population, and are targets for sexual molesters, military recruiters, child traffickers, gangs, and policeman who are charged with getting rid of street children populations.

Going up the pyramid toward the middle of Maslow's Hierarchy of Needs, we see "love and belonging." Maslow theorizes that after physiological and safety needs are met, the third layer of human needs is social, and involves feelings of belongingness. This need is especially present in children. This important aspect of love and belonging consists of friendship, intimacy, and family.

Most street children in Sub-Saharan Africa have witnessed the death of their parents through the AIDS epidemic, and a sense of family and intimacy on this level is now absent. At this point, street children may form relationships with others who are living on the streets in the same capacity. Others may join gangs in order to capture this feeling of belonging and to make up for their lack of family. Otherwise, living on the streets is a very lonely adventure. In Mexico, I observed children clinging to each other in an abandoned building at night just to satisfy that sense of family and belonging. Ten year old girls are having sex in order to feel love in their lives and cure their sense of loneliness.

Another step up the ladder of Maslow's assessment of human needs is the need for respect and to have self-esteem. This is represented by the need to feel respected by others. Without this need being fulfilled, a person might feel depressed, with low opinions of themselves. Street children rate very low on the scale of self-esteem and respect. Often looked down upon by the general population, the police, merchants, and others who view them as trouble makers and waifs, street children tend to have low self-esteem.

At the very top of the pyramid, Maslow presents this feeling of self-actualization, or the satisfaction of knowing that a person has reached their full potential in life. It's a period of creativity and becoming all that a person can be. According to those principles, all of the other layers must be accomplished before this final self-actualization can occur, in which case, street children may never reach that level in their lifetime. If street children cannot meet their basic physiological needs, such as food, clothing, and shelter, it is unlikely that they will reach the next levels successfully, thus making it next to impossible to have their basic human developmental needs met. If a street child is denied a basic education, and is not able to find secure employment, it becomes almost impossible to become self-actualized.

A more likely scenario for a street child is that they will become targets of unscrupulous activists who will recruit them for such things as the "worst forms of child labor," such as child soldiers, or become involved in the sexual tourism business. Once children begin a life of living on the street, they lose most of their safety needs and are unprotected in the larger sense of the word. They become vulnerable populations because they have no one looking out for their well-being. One of the worst forms of child labor is the child trafficking business.

# CHAPTER SEVEN

# CHILD TRAFFICKING

## Child Trafficking

Trafficking in children is a global problem affecting large numbers of children. According to some statistics, there are as many as 1.2 million children being trafficked every year (ILO, 2009). The demand for child trafficking lies in the fact that children are used for work, as cheap labor, and also for the sex trade, as more and more adults will pay for sexual services of children in a form of "sexual tourism."

## Definitions

In November of 2000, the "United Nations Convention against Transnational Organized Crime" was adopted by the UN General Assembly, and with it two new protocols—one on smuggling migrants, and the other trafficking in persons. According to the Protocol, trafficking is defined as follows:

(a) The recruitment, transportation, transfer, harboring or receipt of persons, by means of the threat or use of force or other forms of coercion, of abduction, of fraud, of deception, of the abuse of power or of a position of vulnerability or of the giving or receiving of payments or benefits to achieve the consent of a person having control over another person, for the purpose of exploitation. Exploitation shall include, at a minimum, the exploitation of the prostitution of others or other forms of sexual exploitation, forced labor or services, slavery or practices similar to slavery, servitude or the removal of organs;

(b) The consent of a victim of trafficking in persons to the intended exploitation set forth in subparagraph (a) have been used.

(c) The recruitment, transportation, transfer, harboring or receipt of a child for the purpose of exploitation shall be considered

'trafficking" in persons' even if this does not involve any of the means set forth in subparagraph (a) of this article;
(d) 'Child' shall mean any person under eighteen years of age.

## The Formula

The International Labor Organization, of the United Nations, explains child trafficking in a formula, with a beginning, middle, and an end. The beginning would be a child's original location. The middle would be the "journey" they would have to endure as they are being moved from their original home, and finally, to the end location, or the destination where they will be exploited. The exploitation, of course, can be a variety of different activities. It can exist in the form of agricultural or factory work, child prostitution, or working in the sexual tourism business.

## Supply and Demand

When examining illicit trades of all types, including child trafficking, there is a policy that rules the activity. First and foremost is that trafficking in children is an economic commodity, like sugar, or coffee beans (Moises, 2006). It is driven by the motives of profit. Risk and return are trafficker's primary motivations, and due to the huge profits involved, the benefits to the traffickers outweigh the consequences of jail time or other punishment.

The *demand* for child trafficking lies in the fact that children are used for work, as cheap labor, and also for the sex trade, as more and more adults will pay for sexual services of children in a form of "sexual tourism."

There are many factors that initially create the demand for child trafficking. One of the factors, of course is poverty. As we have already seen, in Sub-Saharan Africa, poverty is one of the major concerns. Areas in which poverty is a problem, plus a population high in street children or orphans, creates the *supply* while the desire for higher profits by greedy entrepreneurs, creates a *demand* for cheap labor, leading to exploitation by those willing to participate in such illegal activities.

Other factors also contribute to the likelihood of child trafficking, such as large populations of orphans, especially in Africa, where there are large numbers of children who have been left homeless due to HIV/AIDS. Homeless children living in refugee camps during times of conflict also become eligible candidates for exploitation, as their parents are nowhere to be found due to war or natural disasters. Children affected by cataclysmic events, such as armed conflict, civil war, famine, or other natural disasters may be targeted for the global sex trade. Some 10 million out of the world's 21.5 million refugees are under the age of 18.

There are also links between poverty, HIV/AIDS, and child prostitution. At the end of 1999, USAID estimated that 13.2 million of the world's children under 15 years of age had lost their mother or both parents as a result of AIDS, and that 90 percent of these children live in Sub-Saharan Africa.

## How Child Trafficking Works

### The Recruitment Process

Child trafficking works by the recruitment process (ILO, 2009). Many times, children may be under a significant amount of pressure to work due to poverty, making them easy targets for traffickers. Unfortunately, much of the recruitment of children is done with the consent of the parents, who sometimes are given an advance payment or they are promised regular stipends from the recruiter.

Other promises are also made, such as telling the children they will receive food, shelter, and often some sort of training or education. Recruiters may also be someone directly involved with the community, as they make money by finding vulnerable children and turning them over to traffickers. In some cases, children may even be kidnapped or abducted by child traffickers, although this is relatively rare.

Child trafficking also involves moving the children to different locations, as is stated in the "middle" portion of trafficking. Sometimes, this can be accomplished by land transportation, such as cars, buses, or trucks. Some countries have open borders, or the lack of security is such that border crossings are made quite easily. Sometimes, the movement can be extremely hazardous, as crossings occur across dangerous environments, as well. Children's lives may in danger as they may not have proper food, water, or medical attention as they are transported to their final destination.

Once a child arrives at their final destination, the actual exploitation begins; this represents the "end" portion of the trafficking formula. As expected, there are many forms of exploitation, depending on their physical size, their sex, their age, and their skill levels. For example, according to UNICEF, children can end up doing agricultural work, factory work, or entertainment venues such as bars and clubs. They may also end up being put out on the streets begging or selling items. Of course, one of the worst exploitations is sexual in nature, as children are sold into sexual slavery or into prostitution rings for the sexual tourism business.

## Who are the Customers for the Global Sex Trade?

A reasonable person may ask how, why, and who it is that participates in this phenomenon known as the global sex trade. Who purchases sex from children, and why do they do it? This is an age old question that demands to be answered. Obviously, pedophiles are the ones who would engage in sex with a child, and this is a universal problem. In the U.S. pedophiles are defined by the American Psychiatric Association's Manual for Mental Disorders:

A person aged over 16, who 'has had repeated, intense, sexually exciting fantasies for a period of at least six months, has had sexual urges or has carried out behaviors involving sexual acts with one or more children (usually under the age of 13).

Furthermore, the fantasies, the sexual urges or behaviors act as considerable impairments in the individual's ability to function socially, professionally or within other important spheres.

## Child Pornography and Commercial Sex with Children

Largely, pedophiles that participate in the global sex trade may have gotten their start by becoming involved in child pornography. Child Pornography is a multi-million dollar business that attracts many followers around the globe. While those who may find themselves interested in commercial sex with children, they may start by viewing child pornography. American federal law prohibits child pornography and describes it as such:

Under U.S. federal law (18 U.S.C. §2256), child pornography is defined as any visual depiction, including any photograph, film, video, picture, or computer or computer-generated image or picture, whether made or produced by electronic, mechanical, or other means, of sexually explicit conduct, where:

- the production of the visual depiction involves the use of a minor engaging in sexually explicit conduct; or
- the visual depiction is a digital image, computer image, or computer-generated image that is, or is indistinguishable from, that of a minor engaging in sexually explicit conduct; or

- the visual depiction has been created, adapted, or modified to appear that an identifiable minor is engaging in sexually explicit conduct.

Federal law (18 U.S.C. §1466A) also criminalizes knowingly producing, distributing, receiving, or possessing with intent to distribute, a visual depiction of any kind, including a drawing, cartoon, sculpture or painting, that:

- depicts a minor engaging in sexually explicit conduct and is obscene, or
- depicts an image that is, or appears to be, of a minor engaging in graphic bestiality, sadistic or masochistic abuse, or sexual intercourse, including genital-genital, oral-genital, anal-genital, or oral-anal, whether between persons of the same or opposite sex and such depiction lacks serious literary, artistic, political, or scientific value.

Sexually explicit conduct is defined under federal law (18 U.S.C. §2256) as actual or simulated sexual intercourse (including genital-genital, oral-genital, anal-genital, or oral-anal, whether between persons of the same or opposite sex, bestiality, masturbation, sadistic or masochistic abuse, or lascivious exhibition of the genitals or pubic area of any person.

Child pornography exists in multiple formats including print media, videotape, film, CD-ROM, or DVD. It is transmitted on various platforms within the Internet including newsgroups, Internet Relay Chat (chat rooms), Instant Message, File Transfer Protocol, e-mail, websites, and peer-to-peer technology.

## What Motivates People to Possess Child Pornography?

Limited research about the motivations of people who possess child pornography suggests that child pornography possessors are a diverse group, including people who are:

- sexually interested in prepubescent children or young adolescents, who use child pornography for sexual fantasy and gratification
- sexually "indiscriminate," meaning they are constantly looking for new and different sexual stimuli
- sexually curious, downloading a few images to satisfy that curiosity

- interested in profiting financially by selling images or setting up web sites requiring payment for access

## Who Possesses Child Pornography?

It is difficult to describe a "typical" child pornography possessor because there is not just one type of person who commits this crime. However, in a study of 1,713 people arrested for the possession of child pornography in a 1-year period in America, the possessors ran the gamut in terms of income, education level, marital status, and age.

Virtually all of those who were arrested were men, 91% were white, and most were unmarried at the time of their crime, either because they had never married (41%) or because they were separated, divorced, or widowed (21%) (Wolak, Finkelhor,& Mitchell, 2005). Forty percent (40%) of those arrested were "dual offenders," who sexually victimized children and possessed child pornography, with both crimes discovered in the same investigation. An additional 15% were dual offenders who attempted to sexually victimize children by soliciting undercover investigators who posed online as minors.

International investigators say foreign pedophiles are usually American or European. Of 160 foreign pedophiles arrested on child sex-abuse charges in Southeast Asia between 1992 and 1994, the largest portion, 25% were American, 18% German, 14% Australian and 12% English.

Up to 40,000 pornographic photographs of children, many from Southeast Asia can be viewed on the Internet, estimates Ron O'Grady, chair of the "End Child Prostitution, Child Pornography, and Trafficking of Children for Sexual Purposes group." According to their annual report, the demand for children in the sex trade is increasing every year, as people from all over the world travel to foreign countries to have sex with children and to take pictures and videos (EPCAT International, Annual Report, July 2008-2009).

## What is Sexual Tourism?

In the manner of this topic, sexual tourism is the traveling to poor countries in order to buy experiences that are forbidden in their own country. This is especially true of those who are looking to have sex with a child. These types of encounters are made possible through a variety of means:

- taking advantage of weak or inadequate child protection laws

- poor law enforcement
- apathetic public officials
- organized crime who provide such activities

In the past, rich and powerful citizens from the western world could travel to countries for the purposes of having sex with children, and even if they got caught, most likely they would just be deported, rather than having charges filed against them. Many times, they could bribe public officials and police officers and could fly back home with no repercussions to speak of.

While the term "sex tourism" gives a picture of an organized tour package operator organizing a trip for European and American businessmen to travel and have sex with children, that is not the case, obviously. Rather, many people (mostly men) travel to poor countries as tourists, and while they are there, seek opportunities to have sex with children. Most of the information is given through informal networks, such as Internet sites, chat rooms, and organizations such as *NAMBLA*, the North American Man Boy Love Association (Davidson, 2005).

One more popular way of obtaining sexual contact with children is through organized sex workers who seek customers for their child sex businesses. They may appear in the form of "street hawkers," taxi drivers, pimps, or provide access through brothels, in which young children are forced into having sex with customers.

## Child Trafficking in Ghana and Sub-Saharan Africa

According to government reports, child trafficking and child prostitution has been a problem in Ghana (Ghana Standard Living Survey, 2007). Child trafficking was both internal and international, with the majority of trafficking in the country involving children from impoverished rural backgrounds. The most common forms of internal trafficking involves boys from the Northern Region going to work in the fishing communities along the Volta Lake or in small mines in the west.

Children from Ghana are reportedly trafficked to neighboring countries to work on farms or in fishing villages. Akateng, a fishing community in the Manya Krobo district in the Eastern region, has been identified as a child-trafficking zone by the Ministry of Women and Children's Affairs. It is estimated that more than 1,000 children are working as slave laborers on fishing boats across the country. The children are usually told they are going to live with relatives who will care for them and send them to school; however, they end up working long hours on fishing boats.

There are also reports of children being given away, leased, or sold by their parents to work in various sectors. Children were also reportedly sold into involuntary servitude for either labor, or sexual exploitation. Ghana is a source, transit, and destination country for trafficked children. Internationally, children are trafficked to neighboring countries for forced labor, and young girls are trafficked to the Middle East and Europe for purposes of commercial sexual exploitation. Girls are also trafficked to Accra and Kumasi to work as domestics, assistants to traders, and kayayeis, porters who trade goods carried on their heads (Human Rights Reports, 2005).

## Trafficking in Labor in Sub-Saharan Africa

In 2000, a survey was taken by UNICEF, and the government of Benin openly admitted that there were as many as 50,000 Beninese children 6-16 years of age working away from home outside the national borders (UNICEF, 2000). The Ivory Coast was the destination for most of the boys from Benin where they were engaging in labor intensive commercial agricultural jobs. The girls were mostly located in Gabon, where they were performing jobs as domestic servants.

A similar study took place in Burkina Faso in 2002, where it was revealed that as many as 83,000 children were working abroad, with approximately 66,000 of them working in the Ivory Coast.

## Child Labor versus Sexual Trafficking

One of the chief differences between child labor as described earlier, and sexual trafficking of children, is the tremendous amount of profit made from the sex trade. Because of the higher profits, more sophisticated groups of traffickers become involved in the movement and the exploitation of children for sexual purposes. These are typically organized crime groups that are involved in other illegal activities as well. They are also able to bribe police and government officials.

Unscrupulous operators recruit children from vulnerable situations and look for their opportunities like war, natural disasters, or other situations. They are promised aid, food, shelter, and education, as well, but may be forced into sexual slavery or prostitution instead.

South Africa has been named as one of the most documented countries involved in sexual exploitation of children. Other countries such as Tanzania, Mozambique, Zambia, Senegal, Kenya, and Nigeria have also been named (Kielland & Tovo, 2004).

A report from the Molo Songololo group, estimates that there are about 38,000 child prostitutes in South Africa, with girls as young as four being sold for sexual purposes. One of the reasons is because of the overarching myth that having sex with a virgin will cure one of AIDS. Children, particularly from Angola and Mozambique, end up as prostitutes on the streets of Johannesburg and Cape Town.

One country in Africa famous for its child trafficking is Nigeria. Nigeria provides neighboring countries with child prostitutes, as well as to Italy and Belgium. Italian police have registered 10,000 Nigerian prostitutes, many of them underage, although other non-governmental agencies estimate the number at much higher rates. A fee of $50,000 will land a girl in Europe, where she will work as a prostitute until she "pays her debts."

## Supernatural Fear as a threat

In some cases, the families of the girls are threatened if they do not comply with the demands for money. In some instances in Nigeria, girls are taken to a shrine, where they are blessed by local shamans, and consequently sworn to silence. According to one girl, they took a lock of her hair, her menstrual blood, pubic hair, and her panties and bra, and then burned them. She was told that if she didn't do what they told her, she would go mad (Kielland & Tovo, 2004). The fear of supernatural punishment keeps the girls paying the traffickers, and prevents them from leaving.

## Long Term Repercussions for Children

Luring children into a life of prostitution is like submitting them to a life of child sexual abuse that they will have no choice but to endure. The ability to lure a child into a sexual relationship is based upon the all-powerful and dominant position of the adult or older adolescent perpetrator, which is in sharp contrast to the child's age, dependency, and subordinate position. In most cases of forced child prostitution, children fall subject to several layers of authority to which they must obey. If we just look at the long term psychological issues of the sexual abuse that occurs, we see that there are many that children will have to cope with.

Children who are sexually abused may suffer from depression, low self-esteem, relationship difficulties, substance abuse, and a host of other complications (F. Porter, L. Blick, & S. Sgroi, 1998). Other studies have shown that sleep disturbances can be a problem, to include nightmares and difficulty sleeping. Victims of sexual abuse may also suffer from anger problems, or even suicidal tendencies (James, B. & Nasjleti, M. 1983).

According to most experts on child abuse trauma, the effects of the sexual abuse of children range from nightmares to suicide, and the degree of harm depends on the frequency, duration, intensity, and nature of the acts. It also depends on the level of the child's development, as well as the child's relationship to the victimizer, the family and the type of support the child receives when the sexual abuse is reported.

## Physical Dangers to Children

The dangers children face as a result of prostitution are both immediate and long-term. Most immediate is the physical, mental, and emotional violence these children experience at the hands of pimps, madams, and customers. Long-term dangers include health problems, drug addictions, adverse psychological effects, and even death. The most tangible consequence for children involved in prostitution is the extremely high probability of suffering violent assault. Not only are child victims of prostitution in danger from street life and pimps who prey on them, but the customers also pose great risks including forced perversion, rape, and physical abuse and beatings.

Children who experience inappropriate sexual activity of a violent or nonviolent nature, are psychologically impacted by a combination of the trauma of the assault itself coupled with the distorted information exploiters use to justify their sexual behavior. Some of the many psychological effects of assault may be revealed through the child suffering from depression, disassociation, and posttraumatic shock (F. Porter, L. Blick, & S. Sgroi, 1998).

Naturally, the number of sexually traumatizing events that were suffered by the child, as well as the length of time during which the child was abused, are predisposing factors to the degree of emotional damage. As might be expected, repeated sexual abuse over a long period of time is likely to be more traumatic than one isolated event. Even so, one should avoid dismissing a single event of abuse as less serious until the circumstances and the child's reactions have been thoroughly examined.

Children that are involved in prostitution and are forced to have sex with adults are in a precarious position, and may likely suffer from a host of psychological and physical problems. Consider the following quote:

"In 1986, when I was sold to a brothel as a prostitute, I was about sixteen years old. Today there are many far younger prostitutes in Cambodia.

There are virgins for sale in every large town, and to ensure their virginity,
the girls are sometimes as young as five or six."

These are the words of Samaly Mam, a Cambodian girl who was sold
into sexual slavery by her grandfather when she was just twelve years old.
For the next decade she was shuttled through the brothels that make up the
sprawling sex trade of Southeast Asia. She suffered nightmares of human
trafficking, where she was raped, beaten, tortured, and forced into
prostitution. She eventually was able to escape with the help of a French
aid worker.

Haunted by her experiences, Somaly Mam, has launched a worldwide
campaign against child trafficking. Her book, *The Road of Lost Innocence*
tells her story in her own words, and reveals the cruel and harsh life of a
child who has been a sex slave (Mam, 2008). Now, as an activist, she has
orchestrated raids on brothels, rescued sex workers, built shelters, started
schools, and founded her own organization to enlighten the world on the
problem of child trafficking. Mam reports that she has rescued girls from
brothels that have been severely punished:

"Girls are chained, beaten with electric cables. They go mad. We've
rescued several children from brothels who have completely lost their
minds."

She also states that in some instances, men will pay over $1,000 to
rape a virgin for a week. According to Mam, a virgin is supposed to give
strength, to lengthen a man's lifespan, and lighten his skin. These girls are
five and six years old, and after the week of raping, Somaly Mam states
that the girls are sewn back inside, without an anesthetic, and resold.

Whether it is in foster homes, residential treatment centers, psychiatric
hospitals, or group homes, or orphanages, children who have been
sexually molested as children may exhibit the following problems:
depression, anger & aggression, low self-esteem, and poor social skills.

## Depression

Almost all child victims will exhibit some symptoms or signs of
depression after the disclosure of sexual abuse (F. Porter, L. Blick, & S.
Sgroi, 1998). The depression may be masked and expressed as complaints
of fatigue or physical illness. Some children may act out their despair
with self-mutilation or suicide attempts (Briere, 1992). A sample of child
and adolescent psychiatric outpatients with sexual abuse histories were

more than four times as likely to have received a diagnosis of major depression as were patients with no molestation history.

## Low Self-esteem and Poor Social Skills

Fear of physical damage, guilt and shame, and the feelings that surround the child during disclosure of sexual abuse tend to undermine the child's self-esteem (F. Porter, L. Blick, & S. Sgroi, 1998). Many of these sexually abused children have been pressured by their parents or caretakers to limit outside relationships, and have relied almost exclusively on interaction with other family members to meet their social needs. Therefore, these sexually abused children often have limited social skills.

## Anger and Aggression

Although some of these children may outwardly appear passive and compliant, most child-sexual-abuse victims are inwardly seething with anger and hostility (F. Porter, L. Blick, & S. Sgroi, 1998). These children are angry at many things in their lives, especially their parents or caretakers for not protecting them from the sexual abuse. This anger may be perpetrated on many people, including school officials, neighbors, friends, classmates, and eventually, those staff members in residential treatment facilities, foster homes, and other treatment facilities.

## Gender Differences in Abuse Victims

### Male Victims

If a male discloses sexual abuse, they might possibly fear that they may be subject to ridicule or worse. Scholars report that the male abuse victim will face several fears if the sexual abuse is disclosed. They may be afraid that they will be labeled a sissy, or unmanly. If a male has been molested by another male, they may fear that people will think they are homosexual. If a woman has abused him, he may just view it as a positive, romantic experience rather than molestation (James, B. & Nasjleti, M., 1983).

## Effects of Sexual Abuse in Boys

One of the most common findings in the literature concerning the effects of the sexual abuse of boys is the presence of a variety of behavioral disturbances such as aggression, delinquency, and noncompliance (Hunter, 1990). Case studies appear to support the empirical literature describing behavioral disturbances in sexually abused boys. Some reported behavioral disturbances in several critical areas, such as fire setting and destruction of property.

Another common problem identified in the literature is some type of sexual disturbance, such as inappropriate sexual behavior, sexual offenses, hyper-sexuality, or gender confusion. In addition, over 81 percent of their subjects exhibited some type of problematic sexual ideation or behavior.

## Long Term Effects

Most of the literature regarding the long-term effects of sexual abuse in males center around the following problem areas: depression, low self-esteem, relationship difficulties, sexual problems (sexual identity problems, and sexual compulsiveness), and substance abuse. Other studies have shown that sleep disturbances, anger management problems, and suicide and other forms of self-destruction often occur in males (Hunter, 1990).

## It's a Business

When considering all the psychological and physical trauma involved with child prostitution at the hand of those who would exploit innocent children, it is important to understand that when all is said and done, it is a business that is generating huge profits. It is a multibillion dollar business globally. According to U.S. government reports, "of the estimated 600,000 to 800,000 people trafficked across international borders annually, 80 percent of victims are women, and up to 50 percent are minors.

Children that are trafficked, either for manual labor or for sexual exploitation have no future. They have no consent, and they have no way out. They are often drugged so that will comply with adult authority. Some are dropped off into destinations where they do not know the language, thus making it impossible for them to communicate to outsiders. Virtually, they become helpless, totally dependent on their abusers, and must remain where they are for their own survival.

This form of child labor is one of the worst forms of child labor. It's harmful to children in the short and long term, and will affect them their entire life. The supply and demand principle is the key to the problem for children in this "worst form of child labor," mainly because of the poverty that has been solidified in Sub-Saharan Africa. Other forms of poverty create the supply for this form of child labor, especially in the regions where there are poor people living in shanty towns, squatter villages, and slums. Like orphanages, these types of residential areas are breeding grounds for exploitation of children. They also create conditions that are harmful to children just by living there.

# CHAPTER EIGHT

# CHILDREN LIVING IN SHANTY TOWNS AND SLUMS

A special report known as the Challenge of Slums, (2003), published by the United Nations Human Settlements Programme (UN-HABITAT), is the first global look at slums and urban poverty. This report was a collaboration of over one hundred researchers, looking at a variety of themes, including case-studies of poverty, slum conditions, as well as housing policies in different regions of the globe.

## Definitions of a Slum

The authors of the "Challenge of Slums report," (2003), defines slums as those characterized by overcrowding, poor or informal housing, inadequate access to safe water and sanitation, and insecurity of tenure.

## The Growth of Slums around the Globe: A World View

According to statistics produced by the International Labor Organization, it is thought that the formal housing market in the developing world rarely supply more than 20 percent of new housing stock, so out of necessity, people turn to self-built shanties, informal rentals, illegal cities and squatter villages. This has also been a constant source of difficulty for a large majority of Africa's children.

All around the world, the growth of slums has been noted. In Asia, for example, experts record that over 200,000 unregistered rural migrants arrive in Beijing every year, many of them crowded into illegal slums on the southern edge of the capital. I personally witnessed these massive migrations while in China in 2010. China has millions of people moving from rural areas to the cities in search of jobs. It is virtually the largest movement of people in human history.

In South Asia, one study shows that 90 percent of urban household growth took place in slums. Of the 500,000 people who migrate to Delhi each year, it is estimated that fully 400,000 end up in slums.

In this process of rampant urbanization, the planet has become marked by the runaway growth of slums, characterized by the definition set out by the *Challenge of Slums* (2003) report, which is overcrowding, poor or informal housing, inadequate access to safe water and sanitation, and insecurity of tenure. U.N. researchers estimate that there were at least 921 million slum dwellers in 2001 and more than 1 billion in 2005, with slum populations growing by a staggering 25 million per year (Challenge of Slums, 2003).

## Africa's Slum Problem

The situation in Africa is even worse. Africa's slums are growing at twice the speed of the continent's exploding cities. For example, 85 percent of Kenya's population is contained in the crowded slums of Nairobi and Mombasa. According to some officials, the UN's Millennium Development Goals for Africa, originally projected to be achieved by 2015 will not be attained for generations. By 2015, Africa will have 332 million slum-dwellers, a number that will continue to double every fifteen years (Davis, 2006). Currently, according to estimates by UN-Habitat, the world's highest percentages of slum-dwellers are in Ethiopia, an astonishing 99.4 percent of the urban population.

Immigrants from the rural countryside in third world countries are making their way to the cities in droves. The individual might be a baby born to a city dweller or an adult migrating from the countryside, but in either case, it's likely that his or her new surroundings will include flimsy walls, disease and an enveloping stench of sewage and trash. The newcomer will have arrived in a Third World slum.

The numbers provided by UNICEF, the principle United Nations organization that oversees the condition of children, are quite disturbing. Poverty in these slums and informal squatter villages and illegal cities has produced a massive problem for children in Sub-Saharan African countries.

## Problems Facing Children Living in Slums

Currently, there are over one billion children living in slums in third world countries that are lacking essential services that are needed for survival and proper development (UNICEF, 2010). Approximately 148 million children under the age of five years are underweight for their age. Another 101 million children are not attending school. There are over 22 million infants in third world countries that suffer from diseases because they have not been immunized. Over 8 million children died before their 5th birthday in 2009. Over 4 million newborns die in the first month of life. There are also 2 million children under the age of 15 living with HIV/AIDS.

An average of 25,000 children under five years are still dying each day, mostly from causes preventable with low-cost, proven interventions. More than 1 billion children are deprived of at least one of their rights in education, water and sanitation, access to information, essential health care, nutrition and shelter.

UNICEF reports that Pneumonia kills more children than any other illness – more than AIDS, malaria and measles combined. Nearly 1.5 million children under five die from the disease each year, accounting for nearly one in five child deaths globally. Currently, 18 per cent of under-five deaths are due to pneumonia, including deaths during the neonatal period (the first four weeks of life).

Prompt treatment with effective antibiotics is critical for reducing deaths from pneumonia. Yet, slightly more than half of children (59 per cent) with pneumonia in the developing world (excluding China) are taken to an appropriate health-care provider. The highest levels of care seeking for pneumonia are found in the Middle East and North Africa (76 per cent), East Asia and the Pacific (excluding China, 66 per cent) and South Asia (65 per cent), while sub-Saharan Africa lags behind at 46 percent. The proportion of children receiving antibiotics to treat pneumonia is even lower.

## Diarrhea

Diarrhea remains the second leading cause of death among children under five globally. Nearly one in five child deaths – about 1.2 million each year – is due to diarrhea. It kills more children than AIDS, malaria and measles combined. Diarrhea is defined as having loose or watery stools at least three times per day, or more frequently than normal for an individual. Although most episodes of childhood diarrhea are mild, acute cases can lead to significant fluid loss and dehydration, which may result in severe consequences – even death – if fluids are not replaced at the first sign of diarrhea. Most diarrhea-related deaths in children are due to dehydration – the loss of large quantities of water and electrolytes (sodium, potassium and bicarbonate) from the body in liquid stools

(UNICEF, 2010). Many well-known child survival interventions are critical to reducing child deaths due to diarrhea. These work in two ways: by either directly reducing a child's exposure to diarrhea-causing pathogens (through the provision of safe drinking water, for example) or by reducing a child's susceptibility to severe diarrhea and dehydration (through improved nutrition and overall health care). Water, sanitation and hygiene programs typically include a number of interventions that work to reduce the number of diarrhea cases. These include: disposing of human excreta in a sanitary manner, washing hands with soap, increasing access to safe water, and treating household water and storing it safely. All processes which are absent in shanty towns, illegal squatter villages, and slums in Sub-Saharan Africa.

## Lack of Essential Services

Living in slums, squatter villages, and other informal or illegal villages lack the essential services such as sanitation and clean water supplies which creates a myriad of problems for children who live there. These conditions make it possible for children to die of such things as diarrhea and the diseases described above. Living in these environments also exposes children to the conditions described below.

## Lack of Nutrition

Undernourished children are at higher risk of suffering more severe, prolonged and often more frequent episodes of diarrhea. Repeated bouts of diarrhea can also undermine children's nutritional status because of their decreased food intake and reduced nutrient absorption, combined with their increased nutritional requirements during repeated episodes. Diarrhea often leads to stunting in children due to its association with poor nutrient absorption and appetite loss. Children living in poverty situations may not get the proper nutrients to deter such things as Diarrhea.

## Stunting in Africa's Children

Stunting in Africa is seen on a daily basis. As I worked in the orphanages in Ghana, I observed that most of the children were experiencing stunting, as well as distended abdomens because of a lack of protein. According to the latest data from UNICEF, the prevalence of stunting in the developing world has declined from 40 percent to 29 percent between 1990 and 2008, but the progress has been stagnant in

Africa. Stunting (low height for age) indicates nutritional deprivation early in life - from conception up to two years of age.

Over the same period, stunting in Africa has only been reduced from 38 percent to 34 percent. Of the 24 countries that account for 80 percent of the world's stunting burden, seven are in the Eastern and Southern African region. Unlike underweight, which is a composite of stunting and wasting (low weight for height), stunting past the age of two is irreversible, and has long-term debilitating effects: children who are stunted are at greater risk of illness and death. It is estimated that countries lose over three per cent of their GDP through the effects of under-nutrition.

# Health Problems in Ghana and Sub-Saharan Africa

## Exposure to Malaria

Malaria poses a tremendous public health problem, especially for children. The World Health Organization (WHO) estimated that in 2009 there were 225 million malaria episodes, leading to approximately 781,000 malaria deaths. While malaria is endemic within most tropical and subtropical regions of the world, 90 per cent of all malaria deaths currently occur in sub-Saharan Africa and most of these deaths are among children under five years of age. Approximately 1 in every 6 child deaths (16 per cent) in Africa is due to malaria (WHO, World Malaria Report, 2010).

The most important sign of malaria is fever. The symptoms in children and adults infected with malaria might also include shivering, severe pain in the joints, headaches, vomiting, generalized convulsions and coma, but also coughing and diarrhea. If children, in particular, are not treated within 24 hours of fever onset, malaria can progress to severe illness often leading to death. Early diagnosis and treatment saves lives and prevents the development of complications. For instance, very high body temperature, drowsiness, convulsions and coma are indicative of cerebral malaria. Jaundice and reduced urine output are signs of liver and/or kidney failure. In most cases, severe anemia is the attributable cause of death.

Today, malaria can be prevented, diagnosed and treated with a combination of increasingly available tools. Controlling malaria is based on both preventing the infection and on prompt effective treatment of the infection and treatment when it does occur. Among the primary tools used for prevention are insecticide-treated mosquito nets (ITNs), indoor residual spraying (IRS) and intermittent preventive treatment during pregnancy.

Sleeping under insecticide-treated mosquito nets (ITNs) is one of the most effective ways to prevent malaria transmission, and studies have shown that regular use can reduce all-cause child mortality by around 20 per cent in malaria-endemic areas. Malaria-infected mosquitoes bite at night, and ITNs provide a sleeping individual with a physical barrier against the bite of an infected mosquito. In addition, a net treated with insecticide provides much greater protection by repelling or killing mosquitoes that rest on the net – an additional and important protective effect that extends beyond the individual to the community. The protective effect to non-users in the community is difficult to quantify but seems to extend over several hundred meters.

## Economics of Malaria for Individuals

The problem in Ghana and Sub-Saharan Africa is that mosquito nets are too expensive for citizens to buy. Poor people living on less than 1.25 U.S. Dollars per day or those that are deemed to be living in absolute poverty or even those living in relative poverty (less than Two U.S. Dollars per day) cannot pay for mosquito nets. During my time working in the orphanages of Ghana, we lost several children to malaria. We left on Friday and came back on Monday, and the children had died over the weekend.

Living in absolute poverty, and living in unhealthy zones such as slums and shanty towns leave residents and children vulnerable to diseases such as pneumonia, diarrhea, malaria, and other problems that may cause death. In developing countries all over the world, children are dying because they can't afford medication, or live in unhealthy situations such as slums.

## Water Supply and Sanitation

Many of the health problems encountered by those living in slums and shanty towns are linked to the water supply—its quality, the quantity available, the ease with which it can be obtained and the provisions made for its removal, once used (Hardoy & Satterthwaite, 1989). Many urban residents are forced to use polluted water from streams or other surfaces which are not clean. It directly relates to millions of deaths of children from diarrhea and other diseases in Sub-Saharan Africa.

When I was in Ghana, young children would approach me on the streets, wanting to sell me bags of water that they insisted was clean and potable. However, it was known that in order to make money, they would bag water from whatever source was available and sell it on the streets.

Even in Ghana, a country that is better off than most West African
Countries is short on potable water for its citizens.

## Removing Waste

Removing and safely disposing of excreta and waste materials is also
critical.  According to experts, over two-thirds of the third world's
population has no hygienic means of disposing of such material.  In
Ghana, this is especially true.

Urban cities in general have struggled against deadly accumulation of
their own waste.  For example, the megacity of Kinshasa, in Africa, with a
population fast approaching 10 million, has no waterborne sewage system
at all.  As Mike Adams delicately points out in his book, *Planet of Slums*,
(2006), people will put their human waste in a bag and toss it wherever
they can.  He labels this activity "flying toilets."  I have personally seen
this activity enacted in South America, as well as Africa.  In fact, in
Africa, at any given time while I was in Ghana, one could smell the
burning of human garbage all throughout the city of Accra, the capital
city, and of course, in rural areas all over Sub-Saharan Africa, people are
disposing of their waste in various ways.  Signs on public buildings even
warn people not to urinate there, which would indicate that this is a
common activity.

## Access to Running Water and Toilets in Ghana

In Ghana, 19.6 percent of households do not have access to toilet
facilities.  Only ten percent of the households have flushing toilets.
According to the report, most households use a pan or a bucket for their
toilet needs, and another 31.5 percent use a pit latrine (Ghana Standard of
Living Survey, 2007).  The situation in the rural areas is even worse, with
only 1.5 percent of households having access to flushing toilets.  In the
same report, only 58 percent of all households in Ghana dispose of their
refuse by public dumping in pits, valleys, streams, rivers, or in the bushes
somewhere.  Another 8 percent of the population burns their refuse, while
another 4 percent buries it.

Every morning, when I would arise to run in Ghana, I would run down
the same roads, but every morning, I would have to dodge a different set
of garbage that had been dumped in the middle of the dirt road.  When it
rained, and that was almost every night during the summer season, the rain
would mix with the refuse causing a horrific odor as the rain spread the
trash over large areas.

Other scholars agree that illnesses related to poor water supplies and poor sanitation have killed more than 30,000 people, and contribute to over 75 percent of the deadly illnesses on the planet (Stillwaggon, 1998). In fact, digestive-tract diseases such as diarrhea, colitis, typhoid, and other types of diseases due to poor sanitation and polluted drinking water are among the leading causes of deaths in the developing world, especially among children and infants in Sub-Saharan Africa. According to other experts, the mortality rate for children under the age of five in Nairobi's slums is two or three times higher than in the city as a whole, and half again as high as in poor rural areas.

When Jeffrey Sachs, one of the worlds' leading experts on poverty and economics first went to Africa, he was amazed at what he was witnessing. After a long career of helping to solve economic problems all over the world, he could not believe what he found in Africa. He was appalled that no one seemed to be offering any medical care for HIV/AIDS, or malaria (Sachs, 2005).

## Shanty Towns:  A Cross-Cultural Comparison

I saw my very first shanty town in Lima, Peru. At first walk-through, I was amazed to see a gigantic black cloud hovering over the dirt road that served as the main thoroughfare through the area known as *Pamplona Alta. Pamplona Alta* is considered the worst Shanty town, or slum in all of Peru. As I got closer to the black cloud, I was stunned with the realization that the cloud was actually a large horde of flies, feeding off the garbage that had been thrown in the streets (Hollingsworth, 2008).

*Pamplona Alta* sits on the sand dunes and surrounding hillsides of the outskirts of Lima, Peru. The neighborhood consists of a shanty town built from mud bricks, wood, tin, cardboard, and almost anything that would serve as potential building supplies. Homes are situated on the hillsides, making them difficult to reach. From the main roads traveled by buses and *Combis*, (minivans that serve a cheap public transit in Peru), a visitor can see dirt paths, and makeshift stairways leading up the hills to the many shacks that have taken root in this area of Lima. This is one of the poorest areas of Lima, and it has been built by homeless people, mostly migrants from rural Peru, and others who had no place to go.

The streets are not paved, and the residents of the *Jovenes* throw their garbage and human waste products into the street. All along the sides of the dirt road that leads through the shanty town, human waste and trash has accumulated in such quantities that wild dogs will race through the streets feeding on the remains. The smell of rotting garbage and human waste lingers and permeates the air and settles over the land, covering it like a wet blanket. The odor of burning trash permeates the air so thick it scorches the lungs.

Some of the older shacks have electricity, but none of them have running water or indoor plumbing. Most of these dwellings have dirt floors, and some have no roof. Most have a roof that consists of rusted pieces of tin or damp cardboard. Water is brought in from the city trucks and they charge these poor citizens as much as they do the suburban wealthy residents of the upper class in Lima who have water piped in.

Poor people dominate the landscape as far as the eye can see in these neighborhoods, living in shacks and structures barely held together in a climate that receives very little rain. Living in shanty towns has become a way of life to most poor people in Lima. Jobs are few and far between, and even when a job is found, it does not pay much, Peruvians say. A good portion of the population of the shanty town at *Pamplona Alta* area receives food from churches or other organizations that are there to help as much as they can, but this is a level of poverty that is considered extreme (absolute).

The shanty town is also riddled with crime. Gangs roam the area during the afternoons and at night, and while we were there working, we were told not to wear anything of value, for pickpockets and muggers were lurking behind corners, waiting for an opportunity to rob us. This was a place where little optimism was present, and no big changes are coming around the pike.

My experiences in Peru, observing and working inside shanty towns such as *Pamplona Alta* are eye opening experiences on how citizens adapt when they are in dire poverty, but still need a place to live. Most housing in the developing world is built "outside the law." Most urban citizens have no choice but to build, buy, rent an "illegal dwelling" since they cannot afford the cheapest "legal" house or apartment. In most cities, 70 to 95 percent of all new housing is built illegally (Hollingsworth, 2008).

## Slums and Shanty Towns in Ghana

Ghana's urban population is expected to double between 2000 and 2015. The majority of new urban dwellers will find themselves living in slum conditions and poorer settlements. In Accra and other towns and cities, competition for land, limited financial and technical capacity amongst local/national authorities and suspicion of those living in informal settlements have combined to worsen problems in poor communities.

Like most slum dwellers around the world, Ghana's urban poor struggle with issues of secure land, poor housing, sanitation, infrastructure, fires, and flooding, as well as threats of forced evictions.

Currently, in Ghana, out of a population of 25 million, approximately 4.8 million residents live in slums. In Ghana, that means that 45 percent of the urban residents live in slums or shanty towns. Most of these residents live in the greater Accra region, the capital city. One of those slum areas is called Jamestown.

Jamestown is one of the oldest regions in Ghana, and was first populated by the British. Adjacent to the old James Fort, the lighthouse overlooks the seaside slum of Jamestown, where numerous fishing boats are based, and despite the desperate conditions of the area, it has become a rather heavily visited area, due to the Colonial history surrounding the region. This area is mostly occupied by the Ga speaking people of Ghana.

Jamestown is a large slum, adjacent to the sea, where many of the slum's residents obtain work on fishing vessels. The slum itself is a highly populated area of hovels, lean-tos, shacks, and dilapidated buildings occupied by many citizens who live without running water, electricity, or any modern conveniences. Dogs, chickens, and goats run through the community, while garbage is thrown everywhere, as there is no garbage collection available. Cooking is done outside on the ground or inside, where smoke quickly fills the places of residence.

Cross-culturally speaking, slums in Africa are not much different from those in Latin America. Sanitation problems is an issue for all, as well as the lack of garbage collection, sewage control, and living without such things are running water, or electricity. Children forfeit going to school to try and obtain work to support their families. Obviously, the bulk of citizens living in shanty towns and slums don't make enough money to send their children to school, therefore, most of the children receive little education.

One of the downfalls of living in poverty, especially in an illegal city, such as a shanty town or a squatter village, is that education gets ignored altogether. Another downfall of living in an illegal city is that the infrastructure is poor. Roads are not built by the city, so dirt roads become the order of the day. There are other problems, as well, such as no running water, no electricity, no phone lines, as well as any sewer facilities or sanitation to speak of because the city provides very few services to those slums and shanty towns.

# Hazards of Living in Illegal Cities

## Lack of Security

Besides the lack of services, there are other concerns with living in an illegal city. Law enforcement becomes a problem, as police will not respond to calls in most areas that are outside the purview of their domain, even if someone were to have the means to call the police. The same is true of the fire departments and other legal services. Since these shanty towns are considered 'illegal," they remain outside of any legal jurisdictions, therefore receive very little services from the city itself. In some shanty towns, crime runs rampant, and with very little support from the police, it is left up to the population within the shanty towns to police the area (Hardoy & Satterthwaite, 1989).

## Geological Hazards and Environmental Concerns

There are other problems, as well, that result from living illegally in shanty towns. One is that the environment of most shanty towns lies in dangerous zones that are not suitable for human habitation. Since most shanty towns are built illegally, oftentimes, they are built in hazardous areas. Many of the places that poor people live are "dangerous areas" where pollution and other hazards often exist (Davis, 2006). For example, Johannesburg's shanty town periphery conforms unerringly to a belt of dangerous, unstable dolomite soil contaminated by generations of mining. At least half of the region's non-white population lives in informal settlements in areas of toxic waste and chronic ground collapse.

Almost every third world city has a district of slums shrouded in pollution and located next to pipelines, chemical plants and refineries. It is virtually always the poorest groups who suffer most from the floods, landslides or other "natural" disasters which have become increasingly common in cities of the developing world. Such zones may be the only places where poorer groups can find to live without fear of eviction (Hardoy & Satterthwaite, 1989).

## Threat of Fires

One of the biggest threats to slum dwellers is the danger of a fire. The basic structure dominating the theme of slums, informal housing, and squatter villages makes it a prime target for fires. In Sub-Saharan Africa, people cook on open fires so often that an accident is bound to happen from time to time. When it does, the nature of the structure of most residences are at risk due to being made from such things as scrap wood, cardboard boxes, and other flammable substances. In most cases, slum fires spread quickly, destroying everything in its path.

Since most slums don't receive services, firefighting services are generally slow to react to such fires, if they respond at all. Even so, the narrow lanes and poor infrastructure of the slum itself would prevent a rational response by fire fighters.

In 2004, a fire swept through a slum in Nairobi, leaving over 30,000 people homeless. In 2005, in Nairobi, Kenya, another fire destroyed over 414 homes, leaving another 1500 people homeless (Davis, 2006). In 2004, a fire left 5000 people homeless in Lagos, Nigeria after a fire ripped through the slums.

In the realm of social problems of children, just living and existing in a slum in Sub-Saharan Africa puts them at risk of a diverse range of disease, physical harm, and puts them at risk of numerous difficulties that could arise because of fire, crime, or other natural hazards and environmental concerns.

## Other Dangers for Children

Children living in poor areas or slums are more prone to selling their children to those who promise them that they will educate their children, take care of them, put them to work, and make life better for them. The family needs the money, and a transaction is made. The children then enter a life of exploitation where they may be sent off to work in the fishing industries, sex shops, or even transported to other countries where they become virtual slaves.

Slums and shanty towns provide a supply of vulnerable children for recruiters for child soldiering, child labor, and sexual exploitation by immoral individuals who are looking to make some fast money. Children who live in these communities become targets for organized crime, and many times may become impressed by those who are committing illegal acts in order to get ahead in life.

Just living in these environments is hazardous for children due to the many health problems caused by the lack of sanitation, fresh water, and secure housing. Children are dying of diseases, fires, and natural disasters. While Sub-Saharan Africa has its share of shanty towns, illegal cities, and squatter villages, what is the possibility of changing those areas anytime soon? Why is Sub-Saharan Africa so far behind the rest of the world?

Globalization is a world trend that is deemed to bring the world into a higher standard of living. It has done so for China, and some other countries that are participating in the new world order, so what is it doing for Africa? Is globalization helping or hindering the growth of Africa? Will it help to curb the overpopulation of urban areas and help to alleviate some of the problems that children are facing in Sub-Saharan Africa?

# CHAPTER NINE

# GLOBALIZATION AND SUB-SAHARAN AFRICA

## What is Globalization?

Globalization is the new economic system on the planet, replacing the Cold War as the new world order. It has brought countries together, and at the same time, made the world smaller. Through the use of some highly sophisticated technology and scientific advances, the world has been brought together in many different ways.

Satellite technology, as well as the rapid advancement of cell phones, fax machines, and personal computers has created a world where information is accessible to almost anyone. Add such recent inventions such as the Internet, and you have created a world in which anyone can take part in the new global system if they have the right tools. Technology such as fiber optics, digitization, and other methods of mass storage capabilities has catapulted this rapid change in our society.

We know that globalization is not just the springing up of new McDonalds everywhere. Rather, it is a new world order. It replaced the old world order, the Cold War, which according to all accounts, ended with the fall of the Berlin Wall in 1989. This represented the golden years of the Reagan Administration in the United States, and Britain's Margaret Thatcher, along with "Trickle down Economic" theory. The Cold War had been the driving force in the world since 1945, but in the 1980's, with rising technology, and other technological advances, the world would be tied together in a very different way (Friedman, 2000).

As Thomas Friedman so delicately points out in his excellent treatise on globalization, this particular era was ushered in by American power, and just as important, the American Navy, which kept the sea lanes open for trade. It was largely America that forged ahead with this new International System we call "globalization." It was America who first enacted the IMF (The International Monetary Fund), GATT (General Agreements on Tariffs and Trade), and encouraged worldwide free trading.

The Cold War itself, in many ways had many of its own rules, such as nuclear weapons, nuclear annihilation, and each country was separated into one of several camps: Communism, Western Capitalism, or neutrality. Each country also based its economy on developing its own exports, and its own national industries. Capitalist countries, such as the United States, based their economies on regulated trade.

While the Cold War International system chopped the world up into many separated pieces, and isolated countries into one of the old camps, the new system of Globalization focuses more on "integration." Today, because of technology such as the Internet, and personal computers, the world is more "interconnected" than ever. It is situated around one key feature: *free market capitalism.* The idea is for countries to let market forces rule, so that their economies will become more efficient, and wealthier. Globalization today, means that free market capitalism will be spread across the globe.

Globalization, like the Cold War, is also defined by its own new rules. Where the Cold War was ruled by nuclear weapons, globalization's rules are opening, deregulating, and privatizing the economy in order to make it more competitive and attractive to foreign investment.

Scholars and experts often disagree on the benefits of globalization. Thomas Friedman, one of the world's most respected journalists has written extensively about globalization, and for the most part has been a proponent of the system. Other scholars, such as the notable MIT professor, Noam Chomsky disagrees, and claims that the rich get richer and the poor get poorer (Chomsky, 1999). The understanding is that these policies are advanced by the interests of the wealthy investors and large corporations. Chomsky refers to these policy makers as *neoliberals,* and their ideas are to encourage private enterprise and consumer choice, all the while, dismantling any social programs or environmental regulations. The result, according to Chomsky, is an increase in social inequality around the globe, and a bonanza for the rich.

Whether one is for or against the policies of the Neoliberals, and globalization, the reality is that globalization is here to stay. There is only one global market today, and the fact is, that countries must expand free trade, democratize their governments, and seek out multinational corporations to invest in their country if they want to participate in this new global order.

Supporters of globalization suggest that free trade leads to a more efficient allocation of resources, with all countries involved in the trade, benefiting. In general, they claim that this leads to lower prices, more employment, higher output, and greater consumption opportunities.

Proponents of globalization say that as more money is poured in to developing countries, there is a greater chance for the people in those countries to economically succeed and increase their standard of living. But, how have these policies affect the children around the world? Has globalization really decreased poverty around the world, or the social problems of children in the third world? Has globalization really reached Africa?

While the fall of the Berlin Wall was a major event in the establishment and indoctrination of the new globalization era, there are other events that drive the process of globalization, and one of those forces of change was the advancing technology. Several new technological changes have occurred, which has revolutionized the world, and brought the world together in innovative ways.

Computerization was one of those driving forces. Computers have changed our world. With computers, now, we can communicate faster and better, and with the invention of the Internet, information is only a key touch away. Prices of computers are manageable by most people, and almost everyone has a computer or a laptop today. But, along with computerization, have come some major advances in technology, such as *miniaturization, digitization,* and *compression technology.* These technologies made it possible to store more information into smaller spaces.

Satellite technology and communications has also improved, along with using advanced fiber optic cable systems for faster, cheaper, and more improved communications. Today's advanced smart phones are more capable than ever, and are more like miniature computers with incomprehensible abilities for retrieving information at our fingertips.

How does this newer and more advanced technology make globalization possible? First of all, it connects us to millions of people around the world, and makes it possible to exchange information at a rapid rate. Secondly, it makes it possible for businesses to operate on a global exchange much easier and faster.

In a sense, technology has found a way to lower the barriers to most countries. When I was in Africa, I lived in a small fishing village, and every day, I would make my way through the dirt roads of the village to the small Internet Café a couple of miles away. It seems that everywhere I have been in South America, Africa, Asia, or Europe, there are ways to get information about the world, just at your fingertips. In some countries, the technology was not as modern, but it was there.

When I was visiting the United Nations Millennium Village in Bonsaaso, West Africa, they had difficulties with acquiring such basic services as running water, or electricity, but at the same time, they were managing to get and use cell phones. Cell phone towers peaked above the canopy in jungle villages where they couldn't even afford to buy food.

So, in a sense, the technological breakthroughs have shrunk our world, brought us together, and given us a chance to play on a global scale. A person literally is connected to the rest of the world through a home computer, a television set, the Internet, and a cell phone. Governments are also included in this moment. It becomes impossible for governments to control information, or lie to their people about how the world is. Through the sense of information gathering and exchange, the truth is always at the tip of our fingers.

## The Golden Straightjacket

Thomas Friedman has indeed changed our vocabulary with his definitions and explanations. When it comes to fully understanding globalization, it is almost imperative to include Friedman's rules of globalization he calls "the Golden Straightjacket." In a sense, he refers to these rules as not just attributes of globalization, but necessary elements for countries to enter this new world order (Friedman, 2000).

As already stated, Ronald Reagan and Margaret Thatcher were at the heart of establishing the Golden Straightjacket. It becomes a method of economic sustenance and methodology for governments once they decide to participate in this new global phenomenon. In other words, countries must put the jacket on to participate in this globalized economy. There are a number of rules a country must follow once they decided to globalize. First, they must open their markets to foreign trade and drop restrictions, tariffs, and barriers. Secondly, they must privatize their economy, making the private sector the main emphasis in the economy. These rules are closely followed by maintaining a balanced budget, increasing exports, and deregulating its own economy.

The general idea is that once a country puts on the Golden Straightjacket, their economy will grow, and their politics will shrink, or even change. It should foster more growth, and higher average incomes— through more trade, foreign investment, privatization, and more efficient use of resources under the pressure of global competition.

In the days of the Cold War, financial markets were as much as cordoned off at the border of each individual country. However, in today's marketplace, thanks to the technological innovations already mentioned, and the deregulation of markets, investing became as easy as punching a few keys on a computer. There are private investors, and there are the multinationals, all with the ability to buy stocks, bonds, mutual funds, and basically invest in the markets of different countries. Since the 1970's, according to the US Treasury, nearly $1.3 Trillion in private capital has flowed to the emerging market economies, which according to experts has increased the capital for growth in many countries.

As an example of the wide range of choices for investors, there are many major markets in which to invest: Eurodollars, U.S. Treasury Bonds, S&P Futures, British Pounds, all the stock markets including most foreign markets such as the Japan index, Singapore, and the list goes on. This new influx of capital has helped poor countries obtain higher rates around the world on their investments, thus bringing more wealth into their countries.

While globalization has produced a various amount of wealth in countries around the world, some will argue that it has also produced some disturbing effects. One of those is the widening of the gap between the "haves and the have-nots." Even in industrialized countries, the gap widened significantly and has remained stable. According to Friedman, there are several reasons for this widening gap: massive demographic shifts from rural to urban areas, rapid technological changes that increasingly reward knowledged workers over the less skilled, the decline of unions, rising immigration into developed countries which drives down certain wages and the shift in manufacturing from high—to low-wage countries, which also holds down salaries (Friedman, 2000).

## Winner Take All Societies

Economists Robert Frank and Phillip Cook argue that this type of system (globalization) also creates inequality (Frank, R. & Cook, Phillip, 1996). For example, those who were already winners do quite nicely in this system, while those who possess inferior skills will do less well. Therefore, largely, the gap between the haves and the have-nots grows increasingly larger.

When we look at these figures internationally, between nations that are developed, and those that are not, we see some alarming results. For example, even though the Internet has spread around the globe, the statistics about who has the most Internet activity still favors the richer countries. OECD countries with only 19 percent of the world's population still accounts for over 90 percent of Internet usage. For example, the United States and Sweden have 600 telephone lines per 1000 people, while Chad in North Africa has one line per 1000 people.

As far as income goes, the figures are also quite unequal. One fifth of the world's people living in the highest income countries have 86 percent of the world's Gross Domestic Product, 82 percent of world export markets, 68 percent of foreign direct investments, and 74 percent of world telephone lines. The bottom fifth in the poorest countries has about 1 percent in each of these categories (U.N. Human Development Report, 1999).

Noam Chomsky, known intellectual, writer, and professor at MIT has stated that the principle architects of globalism, or what he refers to as "Neoliberalism," are the huge corporations that have the means to dominate the world economy as well as influence policy formation (Chomsky, 1999). Neoliberalism, according to Chomsky, is the defining political economic paradigm of our time (globalization)—it refers to the policies and processes whereby a handful of private interests are permitted to control as much as possible of social life in order to maximize their personal profit.

## Cultural Changes

Thomas Friedman commented on some of the cultural changes due to globalization in one of his documentaries. Friedman, (2005), interviewed a number of citizens in India that complained that the younger people were not following the "rituals" of the culture any longer. For example, one leader was complaining about Valentine's Day, which has become a part of their celebrations in India, as the country has become more and more Westernized, or in a better word, "Americanized." Valentines' day, the man recalled, was not in their culture.

Where most experts see globalization changing cultures around the world is in the introduction of American "pop culture." Hollywood dominates the cultures around the globe, thus spreading the culture of America around the planet at rapid rates. This is a phenomenon Sociologists call "Cultural Imperialism." Cultural imperialism is the domination of one culture over another other by a deliberate policy or by economic or technological superiority. Sociologists define culture in the following way: it is the knowledge, language, values, customs, and material objects that are passed from person to person and from one generation to the next in a human group or society (Kendal, 2010). Culture is essential for our individual survival and our communication with other people. We rely on culture because we are not born with the information we need to survive. We must learn about culture through interaction, observation, and imitation in order to participate as members of the group. Culture is also essential for the survival of societies.

One of the chief components of culture is a society's material culture, or a component of culture that consists of the physical or tangible creations (clothing, shelter, art) that members of a society make, use, and share. It is also those resources that are physical that buffers us from the environment. Hollywood can be so influential to other cultures, that they can find their own merging with the dominant culture, thus changing their way of life.

As I have traveled around the world, I saw many people rushing into McDonald's ahead of me. The fact remains, that most people in developing countries want American things, and reach out for them with great enthusiasm. However, it may reach a point where they have lost all touch with their own cultural values. Thomas Friedman refers to this term as "glocalization." He suggests that cultures adopt certain aspects of globalization traits that are helpful and that adds to the overall good of the society without overwhelming it (Friedman, 2000).

## Globalization and Africa

Where does Africa stand in regard to globalization? Has the effects of free trade and capitalism increased the standard of living in Africa? The answer is an obvious and resounding "no." Since globalization actually began in the 1980's, Sub-Saharan Africa has actually increased in areas of poverty. For example, in 1981, just after Globalization began to make its way around the world, Sub-Saharan Africa had 211 million people living on less than $1.25 US per day. By 2005, that number had actually increased to 388 million people.

When we examine the figures of those in Sub-Saharan Africa that are living on just $2.00 US per day, the figures are even more foreboding. In 1981, the Sub-Saharan African region had 294 million of its citizens living on this amount per day. By 2005, even that figure had increased to 556 million (World Bank, 2000).

Why is Africa left behind when the rest of the world seems to be developing and jumping on the bandwagon of a globalized economy? One explanation may be that it's poor markets are not attracting investors. There is little interest in investing in Africa's products or current markets (Giles, 2008). In fact, there has been a global apathetic stance toward Africa for decades, and the fact that globalization is not occurring in Africa, currently, suggests that there still remains a problem. For example, most of the promises made toward Africa, such as forgiving debts, making trade reforms, and improving aid have not materialized.

Although oil has been identified as a resource that the Western worlds want and need, Africa may be revisiting an age-old exploitation, where it is easier to find resources there and take them, rather than investing in the countries themselves. The scramble for Africa's oil is another topic of interest that may be negatively affecting the economies of oil rich African countries.

Africa has always had oil as a natural resource, and its history is quite extensive in selling oil on the world market. In fact, some of the poorest countries in Africa have the most oil, such as Nigeria. While Nigeria suffers from one of the poorest economies on the planet, it possesses one of the largest oilfields. Sub-Saharan Africa has been supplying the crude oil to the international market for decades. Nigeria made its first shipments of oil in 1958, and drilling has been going on there since those days (Ghazvinian, John, 2008).

While oil exists in Africa, it has never produced an economic boom for African countries. First of all, the price of oil plummeted in the 1980's and caused a decline in drilling, and most of the oil wells were abandoned. However, today, elevated prices, changes in technology, and high global demand make Africa a major market for oil production, especially as offshore drilling has become a recent phenomenon due to improvements in deep water drilling. Yet, most of the African nations have not benefitted from this boom in oil production globally. How could that be?

One of the great scandals of the African oil boom is that it has produced far more jobs in the United States and Europe than it has in Africa. Only about 5 percent of the billions and billions invested in African petroleum is spent in Africa. International oil companies often hire their own skilled laborers, generally shunning local populations or companies (Ghazvinian, John, 2008).

Africa also suffers from what is described as the "curse of oil." This phenomenon that suggests that every developing country where oil has been discovered has seen its standard of living decline and its people suffer. Little of the oil wealth trickles down to those who need it the most. This is due to the effect economists refer to as "Dutch Disease."

Dutch disease is an economic condition that, in its broadest sense, refers to negative consequences arising from large increases to a country's income. Dutch disease is primarily associated with a natural resource discovery, but it can result from any large increase in foreign currency, including foreign direct investment, foreign aid or a substantial increase in natural resource prices.

Nigeria, which was one of the richest 50 countries in the early 1970s, has retrogressed to become one of the 25 poorest countries at the threshold of the twenty first century. It is ironic that Nigeria is the sixth largest exporter of oil and at the same time host the third largest number of poor people after China and India. Poverty in Nigeria is in the midst of plenty. Nigeria is among the 20 countries in the world with the widest gap between the rich and the poor.

There are even more repercussions in some of the other major resources in Africa. The diamond mines, for example, have been the source of more conflict than an economic boom for the continent. Conflict diamonds, also known as *blood diamonds* are diamonds that are typically hand-mined within a war-zone, or area of regional conflict, and then sold in the underground diamond market to help finance insurgent activities, civil insurrection, or attempts to invade neighboring territories by rebel armies. The majority of diamond-financed civil unrest has historically taken place along the western coast of central Africa (Angola, Democratic Republic of Congo, Liberia, and Sierra Leone).

As we have seen when discussing the political ramifications of globalization, is that when a country is involved in violent activities such as war, genocide, and other human rights violations, they refuse to put on the golden straightjacket referred to by Friedman. Investors obviously are not going to invest in those countries, so globalization so far has fairly skipped most of the African continent.

## The Effects of Colonialism

It is almost impossible to understand the plight of Africa without understanding some of the early history of colonialism on the continent. Most African countries were carved out of Europe's involvement in the early years of colonialism. Most of these countries never existed before borders were drawn by most colonial powers. In fact, it is difficult to imagine how young most of Africa is, even though its prehistory is older than any other place on the planet.

Most of the earlier colonial powers possessed little more than trading posts along the coastal areas, leaving much of the landmass unexplored and untouched. But later there came an unprecedented scramble for Africa and its natural resources by Europeans from Britain, France, Portugal, Germany, Italy, and Belgium. In the space of a few years, thirty new colonies emerged, and resources such as ivory, gold, peanuts, palm oil ensued, as well as slaves in large numbers.

Then, by the 1950's and the 1960's most of the European powers began to leave and a new era of independence by African nations emerged. The first independence move occurred in Ghana with Nkrumah, Kenyatta in Kenya, Senghor in Senegal, and others who were having a great influence over the African nations. Finally freed from the colonial powers, the nations were free to develop as they could.

These new leaders and nations suffered immediately by major problems. First, the African nations were desperately poor and very ill-equipped to thrive. The colonial powers that ruled did very little to educate the Africans, or to prepare them for their future. In the Congo, for example, it is believed that there were only sixteen people who had completed university degrees at the time of their independence (Bolton, 2007). There was also little infrastructure in most countries. There were few roads or railways other than those used by colonial powers to deliver raw materials for export.

Secondly, there was a lack of national identity in most countries. Only three countries in Sub-Saharan Africa possessed any form of ethnic unity: Somalia, Lesotho, and Swaziland (Bolton, 2007). Other countries were put together at random by European colonials, who had no knowledge of ethnic identity or territorial rival groups. Kenya was a case in point. There are the Kukuyu, the largest and most dominant tribe in the country who were enjoying the enviable position of holding the most power. Then, there were the Masai, who had been split in half, with half the tribe located in Kenya, and the other half in Tanzania, where they became minorities in both countries (Bolton, 2007).

Africa also lacked a workforce that was educated and prepared to take power over their own affairs. This, coupled with desperate poverty, a lack of national identities, and rulers that benefitted from an unprecedented opportunity to increase their own wealth at the expense of their own citizens, left most of Africa in a poor position to enter a globalized market.

The 1960's and 70's saw an increase in corrupt governments, civil wars, military coups, and a host of other problems. Military coups were numerous during those years. For example, Africa experienced forty in the 1960's, 70's, and 80's, along with twelve civil wars (Bolton, 2007).

As the Cold War developed further, most African nations found themselves in unofficial alliances with the Soviet Bloc who was handing out arms and weapons for cash along with western alliances and the U.S. who gave out large loans to shady and corrupt leaders in exchange for loyalty. These situations left African nations with large debts and tons of corruption.

The 1980's marked an unprecedented black mark on Africa, as civil wars dragged on, corruption continued, and those corrupt leaders entrenched themselves in power. Famines became the order of the day in several countries, as the new Structural Adjustment Programs were beginning to be doled out to those nations where large loans had been given. Most of these programs included severe cuts in such things as health care and social services.

The 1990's were another eventful era, as the AIDS crisis loomed. Overall human development in the form of personal income, life expectancy, and literacy began to drop even further. After the AIDS problem approached, human development factors fell in twenty-one countries. By the turn of the millennium, income per person had returned to the 1960's levels. In turn, this desperate kind of poverty means bad health, early death, mothers dying in childbirth, millions of child deaths, constant hunger, and a lack of opportunity, which is still prevalent today.

# Old Continent, Young Nations

It is a fact that most African countries have only been free of the bonds of colonialism for about 40 years. Ghana became the first African country to receive its independence, and that did not occur until 1957. Guinea only gained its independence in 1958. Other countries did not receive their independence until much later. Zimbabwe was 1980, and Eritrea, not until 1993. It stands to reason that they are behind the rest of the world in development, and it also makes sense for such entities of the World Bank, and the IMF to abandon their strict policies that are undermining social programs for children if we are to see any true progress made in those countries.

# Structural Adjustment Programs

Structural adjustments (SAPS) are the policies implemented by the International Monetary Fund (IMF) and the World Bank (the Bretton Woods Institutions) in developing countries. These policy changes are conditions for getting new loans from the IMF or World Bank, or for obtaining lower interest rates on existing loans. Strict conditions are usually set to ensure that money lent will be spent in accordance with the purpose of the loan.

The Structural Adjustment Programs (SAPs) are created with the goal of reducing the borrowing country's fiscal imbalances. The bank from which a borrowing country receives its loan depends upon the type of necessity. The SAPs are supposed to allow the economies of the developing countries to become more market oriented. This then forces them to concentrate more on trade and production so it can boost their economy. However, the realities are something different entirely. Many developing nations are in debt and poverty partly due to the policies of international institutions such as the International Monetary Fund (IMF) and the World Bank, according to expert economists (Sachs, 2005).

These Structural Adjustment Programs have been heavily criticized for many years for resulting in poverty. In addition, for developing third world countries, there has been an increased dependency on the richer nations. This is despite the IMF and World Bank's claim that they will reduce poverty. Following an ideology known as "neoliberalism," and spearheaded by these and other institutions known as the "Washington Consensus" (for being based in Washington D.C.), Structural Adjustment Policies have been imposed to ensure debt repayment and economic restructuring. But the way it has happened has required poor countries to reduce spending on things like health, education and development, while debt repayment and other economic policies have been made the priority. In effect, the IMF and World Bank have demanded that poor nations lower the standard of living of their people (Stiglitz, 2003).

Joseph Stiglitz, Nobel Prize winner for Economics, contends that globalization has indeed helped some countries, but to many in the developing world, globalization has not brought the promised economic benefits. According to Stiglitz, there is a growing divide between the haves and the have-nots, and has left increasing numbers in the Third World in dire poverty, living on less than a dollar a day.

In fact, Stiglitz comments that the actual number of people living in poverty has actually increased by almost 100 million. He points the blame directly on the World Bank, and the International Monetary Fund, which has been tasked with ending poverty around the globe. Today, he argues, the IMF typically provides funds only if countries engage in policies like cutting deficits, raising taxes, or raising interest rates that lead to a contraction of their economy.

The most dramatic of these policies began under the leadership of Ronald Reagan and Margaret Thatcher at the outset of globalization's initial beginnings after the Cold War ended. In the 1980's, the Bank went beyond just lending for projects (like roads and dams) to providing broad-based support in the form of *structural adjustment loans*; but it did this only when the IMF gave its approval—and with that approval came IMF—imposed conditions on the country. The IMF was supposed to focus on crises; but developing countries were always in need of help, so the IMF became a permanent part of life in most of the developing world. Stiglitz has gone or record in saying that the IMF has failed in its mission to help developing countries out of crises. This is especially true of Sub-Saharan Africa.

## Trade Liberalization and Free Trade

*Trade liberalization* is one area that draws a lot of negative attention. Free trade is one of the tenets of globalization. However, Stiglitz argues that opening up markets often fails to live up to its promises, in that Western countries push for open trade for those products they exported, but at the same time continued to protect those sectors in which competition from developing countries might have threatened their economies. In fact, Sub-Saharan Africa the poorest region in the world saw its income decline by more than 2 percent as a result of their trade agreements. There seems to be a double standard when it comes to opening up trade markets.

In some cases, the United States provide subsidies for American farmers that force global prices down, preventing West African cotton farmers from getting a fair price for their cotton. Europe has also been guilty of the same double standards. For example, subsidies on such products as sugar beets are given to Finland and France, reducing the market for African sugar.

## Foreign Investments

Much has been made about the benefits of foreign investments in a country that has decided to put on the Golden Straightjacket of globalization, another of the tenets of globalization. But how does the program really work? In some cases, it has proven to be a key part of globalization. According to the Washington Consensus, growth occurs through liberalization, "freeing up markets." Privatization, liberalization, and macrostability are supposed to create a climate to attract investment from foreign entities. This has been the platform of globalization.

However, in some cases, when foreign businesses come in they often destroy local competitors, quashing the ambitions of the small businessmen who had hoped to develop homegrown industry. Coca-Cola and Pepsi are prime examples, as they overwhelm the soft drink manufacturers in other countries (Stiglitz, 2003).

Mike Davis also illustrates the downside of Structural Adjustment Programs. "In Khartoum," he says that "liberalization and structural adjustment, manufactured 1.1 million "new poor," most out of the decimated ranks of the public sector." He goes on to say that in Abidjan, one of the few tropical African cities with an important manufacturing sector and modern urban services, submission to the SAP regime punctually led to deindustrialization, the collapse of construction, and a rapid deterioration in public transit and sanitation; as a result, urban poverty in Ivory Coast—the supposed "Tiger economy" of West Africa— doubled in the year 1987-88 (Davis, 2006).

As more and more countries disrupt services to the poor, or to social programs, millions of orphans and children are left in institutions where funding has been cut and salaries of professionals have plunged. As more and more funds are taken away from social services programs, and given to development projects and businesses, children are left to starve in poorly run facilities. The impact of these preconditions on poorer countries can be devastating. Factors such as the following lead to further misery for the developing nations and keep them dependent on developed nations:

- Poor countries must export more in order to raise enough money to pay off their debts in a timely manner.
- Because there are so many nations being asked or forced into the global market place—before they are economically and socially stable and ready—and told to concentrate on similar cash crops and commodities as others, the situation resembles a large-scale price war.
- Then, the resources from the poorer regions become even cheaper, which favors consumers in the West.
- Governments then need to increase exports just to keep their currencies stable (which may not be sustainable, either) and earn foreign exchange with which to help pay off debts.
- Governments therefore must:
  - o   spend less
  - o   reduce consumption
  - o   Remove or decrease financial regulations.
- Over time then:
  - o   the value of labor decreases
  - o   capital flows become more volatile
  - o   a spiraling race to the bottom then begins, which generates social unrest, which in turn leads to IMF riots and protests around the world

These nations are then told to peg their currencies to the dollar. But keeping the exchange rate stable is costly due to measures such as increased interest rates. Investors obviously concerned about their assets and interests can then pull out very easily if things get tough.

In the worst cases, capital flight can lead to economic collapse, such as we saw in the Asian/global financial crises of 1997/98/99, or in Mexico, Brazil, and many other places. During and after a crisis, the mainstream media and free trade economists lay the blame on emerging markets and their governments' restrictive or inefficient policies, crony capitalism, etc., which is a cruel irony (Stiglitz, 2003).

When IMF donors keep the exchange rates in their favor, it often means that the poor nations remain poor, or get even poorer. Even the 1997/98/99 global financial crisis can be partly blamed on structural adjustment and early, overly aggressive deregulation for emerging economies. The result is: millions of children end up dying each year.

## Children Die as a Result of SAP's

According to UNICEF, over 500,000 children under the age of five died each year in Africa and Latin America in the late 1980s as a direct result of the debt crisis and its management under the International Monetary Fund's structural adjustment programs (UNICEF, State of the World's Children). These programs required the abolition of price supports on essential food-stuffs, steep reductions in spending on health, education, and other social services, and increases in taxes.

The debt crisis has never been resolved for much of sub-Saharan Africa. Extrapolating from the UNICEF data, as many as 5,000,000 children and vulnerable adults may have lost their lives in this blighted continent as a result of the debt crunch.

## Health Concerns

Even more significantly, the policies of the World Bank and IMF have impeded Africa's development by undermining Africa's health. Their free market perspective has failed to consider health an integral component of an economic growth and human development strategy. Instead, the policies of these institutions have caused deterioration in health and in health care services across the African continent.

As poverty has increased Africa's health problems, World Bank and IMF intervention has also led to a breakdown of health care delivery systems. The role of the state in the provision of health care services has been reduced substantially. Cutbacks in the health sector have severely undermined existing services. And Africa's debt repayment obligations to foreign creditors have diverted money directly from spending on health.

Cutbacks in government spending represent a major component of World Bank and IMF adjustment programs. In the 1980s, real disbursements per person dropped in government expenditure in many African countries. In Madagascar, between 1977 and 1985, government expenditures declined by 24%. Cutbacks in government budgets led to major cuts in the health sector. In the 42 poorest countries in Africa, spending on health care fell by 50% during the 1980s. In Nigeria, per capita expenditure on health fell by 75% between 1980 and 1987 (Davis, 2006).

## The Downside of Privatization

Privatization forms a centerpiece of the World Bank and IMF agenda, and as Friedman points out, it is one of the highlights of globalization (Friedman, 2000). Reducing the size and scope of government, and privatizing state-owned enterprises and services, is a major element of World Bank and IMF programs, as well. Under World Bank and IMF direction, control of health care services has increasingly been transferred from African governments to the private sector. The rationale is that health care services are better financed and more efficiently delivered privately.

The World Bank has recommended several forms of privatization in the health sector. These include: the introduction of "user fees" for health services previously provided free of charge; the promotion of health insurance schemes; increased investments in private care in order to attract patients to private facilities. Through these measures, private services are made the primary focus of health care.

## The Reduction of Healthcare

Throughout Africa, the privatization of health care has reduced access to necessary services. The introduction of market principles into health care delivery has transformed health care from a public service to a private commodity. The outcome has been the denial of access to the poor, who cannot afford to pay for private care (White and Anita Bhatia, 1998).

Ghana was among one of the first African countries where user fees replaced free, or almost free, services. Studies have shown that the introduction of fees led to reduced utilization of these services. Studies in the Ivory Coast have also shown that those with income above the median make more use of medical services when a user fee is charged. But those with below median incomes reduce their use. Across Africa, reports indicate that attendance at hospitals and clinics drops significantly after the introduction of user fees.

Another form of privatization involves the promotion of insurance schemes as a means to defray the costs of private health care. This is inherently flawed in the African context. Less than 10 percent of Africa's labor force is employed in the formal job sector. Therefore, the vast majority of people are not eligible for insurance through their employer. Income levels in Africa are extremely low, and have been reduced further by wage cuts and layoffs associated with World Bank and IMF austerity policies. Most Africans cannot afford the cost of private insurance.

As a result of World Bank and IMF policies, average incomes in Africa have declined and the continent's poverty has increased. Africa's debt crisis has worsened over the past two decades, as the failure of World Bank and IMF intervention has left African countries more dependent than ever on new loans. These institutions have also undermined Africa's health through the policies they have imposed. Forced cutbacks in spending on health care and the privatization of basic services, have left Africa's people more vulnerable to HIV/AIDS and other diseases. As a result, more and more children will be added to the orphan population in Africa over the next several years.

## The AIDS Pandemic

Another major reason that Africa has not developed more rapidly, is due to the HIV/AIDS epidemic prevalent on the Continent. With all other significant events already discussed such as poverty, lack of education, corruption, poor infrastructure and the problems with Structural Adjustment Programs, the AIDS epidemic has become one of the main obstacles to Sub-Saharan Africa's development woes. The disease has touched all areas of life on the Continent, and has restricted growth in many areas.

# CHAPTER TEN

# HIV/AIDS IN SUB-SAHARAN AFRICA

Sub-Saharan Africa is more heavily affected by HIV and AIDS than any other region of the world. An estimated 22.5 million .global total. In 2009 around 1.3 million people died from AIDS in sub-Saharan Africa and 1.8 million people became infected with HIV. Since the beginning of the epidemic 14.8 million children have lost one or both parents to HIV/AIDS, creating large populations of orphans (UNAIDS, 2010).

The social and economic consequences of the AIDS epidemic are widely felt, not only in the health sector but also in education, industry, agriculture, transport, human resources and the economy in general. The AIDS epidemic in sub-Saharan Africa continues to devastate communities, rolling back decades of development progress. The problem for children becomes a major concern in a region beset by so many problems with the epidemic. We have already explored one of the major problems for children: creating orphans. However, there are other concerns that affect children such as creating a shortage of teachers, medical professionals, and other vital services that are cut short because of the epidemic.

## Prevalence in Sub-Saharan Africa by Region

Both HIV prevalence rates and the numbers of people dying from AIDS vary greatly between African countries. In Somalia and Senegal the HIV prevalence is under 1 percent of the adult population, whereas in Namibia, Zambia and Zimbabwe around 10-15 percent of adults are infected with HIV. Southern Africa is the worst impacted by AIDS. In South Africa, for example, the HIV prevalence is 17.8 percent and in three other southern African countries, the national adult HIV prevalence rate now exceeds 20 percent. These countries are Botswana (24.8 percent), Lesotho (23.6 percent) and Swaziland (25.9 percent) (UNAIDS, 2010).

West Africa has been less affected by HIV and AIDS, but some countries are experiencing rising HIV prevalence rates. In Cameroon HIV prevalence is now estimated at 5.3% and in Gabon it stands at 5.2%. In Nigeria, HIV prevalence is low (3.6%) compared to the rest of Africa.

However, because of its large population (it is the most populous country in sub-Saharan Africa), this equates to around 3.3 million people living with HIV.

Adult HIV prevalence in East Africa exceeds 5 percent in Uganda, Kenya and Tanzania. Overall, rates of new HIV infections in Sub-Saharan Africa appear to have peaked in the late 1990s, and HIV prevalence seems to have declined slightly, although it remains at an extremely high level. Just over 3 per cent of the adult population of Ghana is estimated to be affected by HIV/AIDS.

# Overall Impact on African Society

## Life Expectancy

In many countries of sub-Saharan Africa, AIDS has erased decades of progress made in extending life expectancy. Average life expectancy in Sub-Saharan Africa is now 52 years and in the most heavily affected countries in the region life expectancy is below 51 years. In five of the six Sub-Saharan African countries where life expectancy is lower than it was in the 1970s, this decline has been directly linked to HIV/AIDS (UNDP, 2010 Human Development Report).

## The Effect on Families and Economics

The effect of the AIDS epidemic on households can be very severe, especially when families lose their income earners. In other cases, people have to provide home based care for sick relatives, reducing their capacity to earn money for their family. Many of those dying from AIDS have surviving partners who are themselves infected and in need of care. They leave behind children who are often cared for by members of the extended family.

Stephanie Nolan (2007), The African Bureau Chief for Toronto's *Globe and Mail*, tells a story of how she met a family in Malawi early in 2002. The house belonged to a 35 year old woman who was raising five children on her own because her husband was gone. She was plagued by diarrhea and barely had the strength to raise a hoe, although her plot of land was the only source of food for her and her children. The woman also was raising two of her dead sister's children and two orphaned cousins.

In Malawi, one out of every six adults has the disease. Many were earning less as a result of sheltering children whose parents had already died. It was like a downward spiral. If the family earned less, fewer children went to school, and poverty became absolute. The burdens on the families in Sub-Saharan Africa increase daily, therefore increasing the risk of children entering orphanages, being exploited by unscrupulous recruiters looking for child soldiers, or looking for children for cheap labor or for the sex tourism business.

## The Effect on Healthcare

In all affected countries, the epidemic is putting strain on the health sector. As the epidemic persists, the demand for care for those living with HIV rises, as does the number of health care workers affected. Typically, countries with high prevalence have overstretched health systems causing shortfalls in the healthcare sector.

The AIDS epidemic itself contributes to the overburdened health sector. In one study in Kenya, for example, 50-60 percent of public hospital beds were found to be occupied by HIV patients. In most cases, countries in Sub-Saharan Africa that are suffering through the epidemic have seen professionals, such as doctors and nurses dwindle. In Tanzania, for example, there are only 0.02 doctors per 1000 people in the population, and only .37 nurses per 1000 people. Compare these figures to countries like the United States, where there are 2.56 doctors per 1000 people, and 3.06 nurses per 1000 people (Opiyo, 2008).

While AIDS is causing an increased demand for health services, large numbers of healthcare professionals are also being directly affected by the epidemic. Botswana, for example, lost 17 percent of its healthcare workforce due to AIDS between 1999 and 2005. A study in one region of Zambia found that 40 percent of midwives were HIV-positive (UNAIDS, 2009). Healthcare workers are already scarce in most African countries. Excessive workloads, poor pay and migration to richer countries are among the factors contributing to this shortage.

## Effect on Education and Children in School

A decline in school enrolment is one of the most visible effects of the epidemic. This in itself will have an effect on HIV prevention, as a good, basic education ranks among the most effective and cost-effective means of preventing HIV (The World Bank, 2002, Education and HIV/AIDS), but there also effects on teachers who have the disease as well.

There are already numerous barriers to school attendance in Africa, as we have seen when examining schools. Children may be removed from school to care for parents or family members, or they may themselves living with HIV. Many are unable to afford school fees and other such expenses – this is particularly a problem among children who have lost their parents to AIDS, who often struggle to generate income.

Studies have suggested that young people with little or no education may be around twice as likely to contract HIV as those who have completed primary education. In this context, the devastating effect that AIDS is having on school enrolment is a big concern. In Swaziland and the Central African Republic, it was reported that school enrolment fell by 25-30 percent due to AIDS at the beginning of the millennium (The World Bank, 2002, Education and HIV/AIDS).

## Effect on Teachers

HIV and AIDS are also having a devastating effect on the already inadequate supply of teachers in African countries; for example, a study in South Africa found that 21 percent of teachers aged 25-34 were living with HIV. Teachers who are affected by HIV and AIDS are likely to take periods of time off work. Those with sick families may also take time off to attend funerals or to care for sick or dying relatives, and further absenteeism may result from the psychological effects of the epidemic.

When a teacher falls ill, the class may be taken on by another teacher, may be combined with another class, or may be left untaught. Even when there is a sufficient supply of teachers to replace losses, there can be a significant impact on the students. This is particularly concerning given the important role that teachers can play in the fight against AIDS.

The illness or death of teachers is especially devastating in rural areas where schools depend heavily on one or two teachers. Moreover, skilled teachers are not easily replaced. The impact of AIDS in Tanzania for example means that in 2006 it was estimated that around 45,000 additional teachers were needed to make up for those who had died or left work because of HIV and AIDS. The greatest proportion of staff that have been lost, according to the Tanzania Teacher's Union, were experienced staff between the ages of 41 and 50.

According to The Education and HIV/AIDS, "Window of Hope Report, 2010," the effect on the supply of teachers has been ominous. For example, in the Central African Republic 85 percent of teachers who died between 1996 and 1998 were HIV positive, and on average died 10 years before they were due to retire. In Zambia, 1,300 teachers died in the first 10 months of 1998, compared with 680 teachers in 1996. HIV-positive teachers are estimated at more than 30 percent in parts of Malawi and Uganda, 20 percent in Zambia, and 12 percent in South Africa.

# Child Mortality due to AIDS

An estimated 3.8 million children have been infected with HIV since the epidemic began, and more than two-thirds have died.  UNAIDS estimates that in 1999, 570,000 children under the age of 15 became infected, and that 330,000 to 670,000 children under 14 have died of AIDS, the vast majority of them in Sub-Saharan Africa (UNIAIDS, 2000). The majority of children dying of AIDS are young children who have contracted the disease from mother-child transmission.   The statistics show the following scenarios:

- Of children born with HIV because of vertical transmission from the mother, fewer than half survive to school age
- Children born uninfected are unlikely to become infected until they reach adolescence and become sexually active
- Prevalence among 15-19-year-old girls in Africa is often more than twice that of boys
- Older children and young adolescents who contract HIV when they become sexually active are most likely to die in their 20's or early 30's.

## Victims of Sexual Assault

Sexual abuse is common in Africa as well, which leads to another source of contraction of the virus for young girls.  In South Africa, for example, it is estimated that 40-47 percent of sexual assaults are perpetrated against girls aged 15 or younger.  In Zimbabwe, 10 percent of girls reported that their first sexual intercourse was forced.  In South Africa, it is over 30 percent of the girls.  In rural Malawi, where AIDS is extremely pervasive, 55 percent of adolescent girls in a survey reported being forced into having sex.

In urban Zimbabwe, half of all reported rape cases involved girls younger than 15, who were molested by male relatives, neighbors, or schoolteachers.  In one Ugandan district, 31 percent of schoolgirls (and 15 percent of the boys) reported being sexually abused by teachers. A study in Tanzania found that a quarter of primary school girls reported having sex with adult men, including teachers.

# How did HIV/AIDS get this bad?

HIV/AIDS spread over Africa like a wildfire in the 1970's, once it took hold in the communities, according to Stephanie Nolan, (2007), who collected stories of AIDS in her landmark book, *28 Stories of AIDS in Africa*. The trails that the virus used to spread were diverse. We see stories about truck drivers, miners, and soldiers, each spreading the virus due to sexual exploits outside the marriage, then returning to their wives and giving the disease to their spouse.

## Truck Drivers

Most goods and services in Africa are delivered by truck. Goods enter and leave Africa through a handful of major ports, according to Nolan (2007), who spent a great deal of time mapping out this industry and how it affected the spread of the virus. Lagos and Dakar in West Africa are central ports, and Durban and Maputo in South Africa, as well as Mombassa and Dar es Salaam in the Eastern part of Africa. From there, most everything moves along the roads, through the continent into the heart of Africa. Other countries are landlocked, and everything has to be transported in trucks. Most of these countries are located in the center of Africa, such as Uganda, Rwanda, Zambia, Zimbabwe, Malawi, Burundi, and Botswana.

Truck stops at night are filled with truck drivers, and prostitutes abound in each of these areas, desperate to make any money they can. One researcher from the University of Nairobi in the 1980's began to notice the high rate of AIDS among prostitutes and concluded that 80 percent of the sex workers he tested had the virus. After testing their biggest clientele, truck drivers, he noticed that 36 percent of the Ugandan drivers were infected, 19 percent of the Kenyan drivers, and 51 percent of the Rwandan truck drivers were infected.

Currently, according to Nolan, (2007), long-haul truck drivers have an HIV infection rate twice that of the general population, and they remain a key group for the transmission of the disease. Their lives are spent in the environment where prostitutes are numerous, and little stigma is present about utilizing them. Of course, the problem is exacerbated when they return home and have sexual relations with their wives.

The problem in Africa is so bad that a group called "Corridors of Hope" targets drivers at border crossings and truck stops, greeting truck drivers with condoms, education and health care. Most drivers report that they don't like condoms because it ruins the moment for them, and that they do not like them.

## Miners

Another population responsible for the spread of AIDS across Africa is miners. At one point, in South Africa, the development of gold mines had drawn a large migratory population of men to labor in the mines. More than 750,000 men from several countries were beginning to find the mines an important job opportunity. At one time, South Africa's mines workforce was over 80 percent foreign.

Mines in Africa became an important source of income all over the region. In fact, men journey hundreds of miles from Malawi and Lesotho to work in the diamond mines at Kimberly. The same was true of the copper mines in Zambia, and the coal mines of Zimbabwe.

Hostels are set up to accommodate all the workers in the mining regions all over Africa. A professor of medicine at Brown University studied mining workers extensively in Africa, and stated that to create an epidemic, "take as many young men as you could away from their families, isolate them in single-sex hostels and give them easy access to sex workers and alcohol. Then, to spread the disease around the country, you'd send them home every once in a while to their wives and girlfriends."

Research by Lurie, (2003), found that male migrant workers are two and a half times more likely to be infected with HIV than non-migrant workers. Many South African mines report that nearly 30 percent of their workforce is infected, and studies of the women who work the bars or the open-air brothels in the fields outside the mine fence show they have HIV infection rates as high as 80 percent.

Lurie also tracked couples in which one person has the virus and one doesn't, and he found that in two-thirds of those cases, it's the migrant man who is infected. In some cases, the women who have been left alone find partners while the husband is gone, and are also infected.

In Mozambique, the infection rate where most of the miners live is at 20 percent, the highest in the country. However, the country is in no condition to solve the problem. In 2004, there were just 450 doctors working in the entire country. As Nolan (2007), suggests, mining is one of the most important facets of the country's economy, but with staggering rates of HIV/AIDS infections, it has impacted the gold mining business in the form of absenteeism, funeral costs, lowered productivity due to illness, and a host of other factors. So, clearly, migratory mining workers are also contributing to the HIV/AIDS problem in Africa in a big way.

## The Military

Another large contributor to the spread of the HIV/AIDS problem in Africa is the military. Africa's military responds to such things as border conflicts, revolutions, and peacekeeping initiatives across the region. As they are seen as a group with some money to spend, prostitutes seek out soldiers as customers along military camps. In South Africa, seven out of every ten deaths in the armed forces are AIDS related, which has caused a problem with military readiness (Nolan, 2007).

In the same way that the virus is being spread by miners and long-haul truck drivers, soldiers have sexual relations with prostitutes who are infected, and when they go home, they have sex with their wives or girlfriends and infect them.

## Ghana Observations

As I traveled around Ghana, in West Africa, I noticed that the numbers of prostitutes that were walking the highways, and hanging around bars and truck stops was incredibly high. At night, trucks would park near the truck stops and bars, and prostitutes would line up to climb into the cab of a truck, then move on to the next one. The trucks that parked on the side of the roads were so numerous, that it hindered traffic as it struggled to keep moving.

## Prevention

I had numerous conversations with men in Ghana who had been infected with AIDS, and generally, the lack of education seemed apparent. One man told me that when he wanted to have sex with a prostitute, he would see out the ones that were "heavy." They most likely did not have the disease, he told me. Others would tell me that after having sex with a woman that was affected with AIDS, they would jump in the ocean, and the disease would be washed away.

I was also interested in what prevention was being taught in the schools about prevention of the virus, and found very little actual information available. All the talk about how information was being given to children was mostly false, or misleading. About the only prevention information I saw in Ghana was signs around the city of Accra. One of the signs meant for young schoolchildren read: "Turn your back on AIDS," and it showed two grown women with their backs turned. In the middle of the sign, it said, "Stop AIDS." At the bottom of the sign, it read, "Be faithful to your partner." This was a sign meant to educate young school children in primary school.

When all factors are considered, Sub-Saharan Africa's problem with the HIV/AIDS epidemic is one of the glowing reasons they are not advancing as much as they could. It has crippled the critical elements of society, including families, economics, the health care system, education, as well as the overall workforce of the country. Africa is losing the most valuable commodities, as well, their children, which are the future of Africa. Without hope of an education, the workforce will continue to wither away, further debilitating the continent. Orphans will continue to plague Africa as well, which gives way to a vulnerable population to such things as recruiting child soldiers, child prostitutes, child laborers, and a host of social problems already discussed in this book.

# CHAPTER ELEVEN

# MILLENNIUM VILLAGE PROJECT

It was a journey that I would remember forever. We started out on a bus ride from Accra, the capital city of Ghana, and rode toward Kumasi, the second largest city in Ghana. Our mission: to visit and observe the Millennium Village Project in Bonsaaso. I had two students with me, one a law student, and the other a Political Science undergraduate student from Canada. All of us had met and had worked together with orphanages and other projects in Ghana.

The Millennium Villages project is a project of the Earth Institute at Columbia University, the United Nations Development Program, and Millennium Promise. The goal of the program is to eradicate extreme poverty, based on the eight millennium goals set by the United Nations (*The Earth Institute*, Columbia University, 2011).

The Millennium Development Goals (MDGs) are eight international development goals that all 192 United Nations member states and at least 23 international organizations have agreed to achieve by the year 2015. These goals are:

- Eradicate extreme poverty and hunger
- Achieve universal primary education
- Provide gender equality and empower women
- Reduce child mortality rates
- Improve maternal health
- Combat HIV/AIDS, malaria and other diseases
- Ensure environmental sustainability
- Develop a global partnership for development

The MDG's provide concrete, numerical benchmarks for tackling extreme poverty in its many dimensions. The MDGs also provide a framework for the entire international community to work together towards a common end – making sure that human development reaches everyone, everywhere. If these goals are achieved, world poverty will be cut by half, tens of millions of lives will be saved, and billions more people will have the opportunity to benefit from the global economy. The Earth Institute developed the programs in the Millennium Village Project with these eight goals in mind.

The Institute is under the direction of Professor Jeffrey D. Sachs, and comprises more than 30 research centers and some 850 scientists, postdoctoral fellows, staff and students. The Institute studies and helps to create solutions for problems in public health, poverty, energy, ecosystems, climate, natural hazards and urbanization.

I was specifically interested in observing the social problems of children living in the rural areas of Ghana, and trekking out to Kumasi and the tribal zones was one way to do that effectively. The Millennium Promise Village proved an interesting visit and chance to observe a humanitarian project that seemed to be doing well according to most reports.

The Millennium Promise works specifically in Africa, and currently, there are ten countries with Millennium Villages. They utilize simple solutions like providing high-yield seeds, fertilizers, medicines, drinking wells, and materials to build school rooms and clinics. The Bonsaaso project was obviously on my list to observe while in Ghana. I had no idea what I had gotten myself into.

## Kumasi and the Ashanti Tribe

Kumasi is the second largest city in Ghana, and is the Ashanti Tribal Region of Ghana, home of the once majestic Ashanti Tribe. The government of Ashanti is shaped like a pyramid. There is one king and he heads the Ashanti Confederacy Council, a group made of paramount chiefs. A paramount chief presides over district chiefs. A district chief presides over a District Council of Elders, which is made up of sub-chiefs. Villages are brought together by a sub-chief (U.S. Department of State, June 1, 2011. Bureau of African Affairs: Ghana).

The Ashanti tribe of the Akan is the largest tribe in Ghana and one of the few matrilineal societies in West Africa (Briggs, 2007). Once renowned for the splendor and wealth of their rulers, they are most famous today for their craft work, particularly their hand-carved stools and fertility dolls and their colorful Kente cloth. Kente cloth is woven in bright, narrow strips with complex patterns; it's usually made from cotton and is always woven outdoors, exclusively by men.

The Ashanti religion is a mixture of spiritual and supernatural powers. They believe that plants, animals, and trees have souls. They also believe in fairies, witches, and forest monsters. There are a variety of religious beliefs involving ancestors, higher gods, or "*Abosom*," and '*Nyame*', the Supreme Being of Ashanti. The Ashanti also practice many rites for marriage, death, puberty, and birth (Fisher, 1998).

To the Ashanti, the family and the mother's clan are most important. A child is said to inherit the father's soul or spirit (ntoro) and from the mother a child receives flesh and blood (mogya). This relates them more closely to the mother's clan. The Ashanti live in an extended family. The family lives in various homes or huts that are set up around a courtyard. The head of the household is usually the oldest brother that lives there. He is chosen by the elders. He is called either Father or Housefather and is obeyed by everyone.

Boys are trained by their fathers at the age of eight and nine. They are taught a skill of the fathers' choice. The father is also responsible for paying for school. Boys are taught to use the talking drums by their mothers' brother. Talking drums are used for learning the Ashanti language and spreading news and are also used in ceremonies. The talking drums are important to the Ashanti and there are very important rituals involved in them. Girls are taught cooking and housekeeping skills by their mothers. They also work the fields and bring in necessary items, such as water, for the group.

Marriage is very important to Ashanti communal life and it can be polygamous. Men may want more than one wife to express their willingness to be generous and support a large family. Women in the Ashanti culture will not marry without the consent of their parents. Many women do not meet their husbands until they are married. Even so, divorce is very rare in the Ashanti culture and it is a duty of parents on both sides to keep a marriage going.

The ancient capital of the Ashanti kingdom, Kumasi is still the heart of Ashanti country and the site of West Africa's largest cultural center, the palace of the Ashanti king. To add to the appeal, it's surrounded by rolling green hills and has a vast central market as vibrant as any in Africa.

# The Journey

The bus ride from Accra to Kumasi was a 250 Kilometer trip, and I sat by the window, watching the African countryside flash by. I was always amazed at the diversity of the landscape in Ghana, with the mountains, and the rainforest. I was anxious to visit Kumasi, as it had such a vibrant history and culture.

Once we arrived in Kumasi, we booked a small room in a hostel central to the shopping districts of Kumasi. There was only one bed, but the management was able to throw a mattress on the floor for me. It reeked of an odor I did not want to identify. Of course, there was only one bathroom on our floor, and there was no running water, which was typical of Ghana, unfortunately.

We spent a good portion of the morning walking around Kumasi observing and trying to find someone who could take us out to the Millennium Village in Bonsaaso. We had no idea how difficult this would be. Bonsaaso is located in the Amansie-West District of the Ashanti Region of Ghana. We finally found a *Tro-Tro* driver who said he could take us out to the Amansie-West District. The area is in the middle of a thick rainforest and it would be a bumpy ride out to Bonsaaso.

The *Tro-Tro* bounced along the dirt roads for what seemed like hours before he stopped the vehicle and motioned for us to get out. We quizzed him about where the village was located and he pointed down the long dirt road in front of us and took off, leaving us standing in the middle of the dirt road. We began walking, not knowing exactly where we were going, or how far the village was. We were surrounded by thick rainforest and thick vegetation on both sides of the road. A few miles ahead, we spotted a sign. We had arrived at the headquarters of the Millennium Village in Ghana. The Bonsaaso project consisted of a cluster of six villages, with a total of 30,000 people spread out over a wide area of the rainforest. Most of the area is made up of small rural farms on rather small plots of land. Most of the farmers are growing small cash crops and are not able to grow crops for their own subsistence. Most of these villages are isolated and travel, as we found out, is very difficult because of the dirt roads and lack of infrastructure. When it rains, the roads are largely impassable.

As we sat down with the manager of the project, I was amazed to find out how invested and deeply involved the people in each community were to this project. This is not a hand out, this is definitely what I call a "hand up." Most of the information below is available on the Earth Institute website.

# How the Project Works

## Eradicating Extreme Poverty and Hunger

Each Millennium Development goal is addressed in each project. Addressing the first goal (eradicating extreme poverty), the project has made improvements to the village agricultural capacities by using many advanced techniques of scientific farming. By utilizing fertilizers, high yield seeds, and other advanced techniques, the project has increased the agricultural yields of crops such as maize, which has gone a long way in ending such things as malnutrition. In Bonsaaso, for example, the following improvements have been seen according to the Earth Institute:

- Average maize yields increased from 2.2 to 4.5 tons per hectare
- Chronic malnutrition has decreased by 27 percent among children under two
- Development of a community-based management team has supported management training, links to credit, and transport of products to local markets
- Number of farmers contributing to the school meals programs increased 10 fold from 2009 to 2010 (over 3,000 farmers)
- More than 600 vaccinations were provided to sheep, goats and poultry

## Achieve universal primary education

Originally, one of the main problems in this area was that there were not enough primary schools to support the population of the village cluster. Children were required to walk several miles to attend schools because of the distances and the lack of transportation. Schools were remote and sparsely supplied with resources and materials. Teachers were almost nonexistent, as well. By addressing the problems of education in the area, the following improvements have been seen in the Bonsaaso project:

- 56% of primary school students now receive a daily school meal, up from less than 1 percent
- 52 classrooms have been refurbished
- Schools have been connected to the electricity grid
- Continued construction of gender separate latrines
- Training has reached 61 teachers and housing is being built for them
- Collaboration with CARE is working on an education project focused on girls

It was amazing to learn that school attendance had increased simply on the idea of having school lunches for children. This had a positive effect for various reasons, all of them good.

## Health Needs

Health problems in Bonsaaso were extreme. They were dealing primarily with Malaria, as well as HIV/AIDS and other difficulties. There were very few functional health facilities in the entire cluster and community members had to travel between 2 and 40km to access health care. There was also a lack of qualified medical staff, or sufficient transportation to travel to the closest clinic. One of the most important additions to this cluster was the recent purchase of a new ambulance. We walked around the ambulance several times, as the manager showed me the ins and outs of it. Other improvements have also been made, including the following:

- Completion construction or rehabilitation on 6 of the 7 clinics required to meet cluster needs
- 61 percent of births are attended by skilled health personnel, double from baseline levels
- 86 percent of women have at least 4 antenatal care visits, up from 50 percent
- Threefold increase in HIV testing
- Community health workers supplemented with additional staff and training
- Salaries have been raised to attract and retain health workers

## Further Progress in Obtaining MDG's

Other problems addressed by the project included their access to clear and safe water, as well as sanitation and accessibility to electricity and improved infrastructure. When children have to sit in the dark when the sun goes down, they cannot study effectively for school projects or homework. Having electricity can also mean access to such things as computers and other electronic devices which increase learning capabilities.

The project has reported the following progress in Bonsaaso:

- Access to safe water sources doubles from 41 percent to 89 percent
- Initiation of cost-sharing program has increased access to improved sanitation: Access to improved sanitation increased from 4 percent to 60 percent
- Ownership of mobile phones has increased from 4 percent to 30 percent

- MVP worked with government to repair 219 kilometers of roads and construction of 162 culverts under the government's routine maintenance program
- 8 communities are now connected to the national electricity grid, up from 0
- Solar photovoltaics was installed in clinics to ensure off-grid access

# A Year by Year Approach

The programs in most of the Millennium Village Projects usually begin with a case study and meetings that require the attendance of the citizens of the communities that are involved in the startup. All members of the communities have to contribute to the funding of the program. In each case, the program follows a year-by-year approach to implementing the strategies in the projects. The following strategy is taken from the Millennium Village Project website:

## YEAR 1

**Key Activities:**
- Distribute subsidized fertilizer and improved seeds and train farmers in improved techniques
- Distribute long-lasting, insecticide- treated bed nets and provide training on proper use
- Begin rehabilitation and construction of schools, health clinics and water points

**Outcomes:**
- Increased food security through increased staple crop yields
- Decreased prevalence of malaria
- Improved key facilities

## YEAR 2

**Key Activities:**
- Introduce crop diversification and link farmers to local markets for crop sales
- Expand locally-sourced school meals program using new crop surpluses

- Expand disease control for HIV/AIDS, malaria, tuberculosis and other tropical diseases

**Outcomes:**
- Increased production of higher value and more nutritious crops
- Increased school attendance
- Reduced child mortality and maternal mortality rates
- Improved health care and disease control

**YEAR 3, 4, 5**

**Key Activities:**
- Expand access to agricultural finance and promote business development
- Extend the electricity grid (where possible) and introduce alternative energy sources
- Construct and maintain roads
- Initiate piped water systems and large scale irrigation projects
- Establish and improve mobile telephone and internet connection

**Outcomes:**
- Increased self-financing of agricultural inputs
- Growth in local business and entrepreneurship
- Greater access to energy, improved transport and information and communication technologies (ICT)
- Make progress towards reducing child and maternal mortality, improving education, environment, health, gender equality and water

## What does it Cost?

The funding for the project is a shared effort. There are donors, Non-Governmental Agencies that get involved, as well as the local and national governments and the village itself. The funding breaks down the following way according to the information from Millennium Village Project sources: each Millennium Village budgets an investment of $120 per person per year. Half of this is mobilized directly through the MVP initiative, and the other half comes from partners, including the community itself ($10), the national government ($30), and NGO partners ($20). Given the trends in global inflation, the total cost in 2010 might reach approximately $160 per capita. Despite this the MVP has continued to work within its own budget.

## Impressions

I left the Bonsaaso project feeling satisfied that at least in one corner of the world, a project is actually helping instead of hindering. I was impressed by the enthusiasm of the people who resided within the communities of the project. They were anxious to see more improvements in their lives and situations, and are working hard to alleviate some very serious problems.

I was also impressed that this was not a "handout" program, but a "hand up." Every citizen in the community has to participate in some way, giving the program a jump start from the very first moment.

## Other Millennium Village Sites

There are nine other sites for the Millennium Village Project in Africa. They are located in Koraro, Ethiopia, with 11 villages in the cluster and over 67,000 residents. Sauri, Kenya, was the very first project site, and contains a cluster of 11 villages and 65,000 people.

Derfu, Kenya is another location with only one village of 6,000 people. The vicious cycle of poverty is due to multiple and complex interwoven problems including acute food shortages as a result of recurrent droughts, unreliable and erratic rainfall, subsequent floods with outbreaks of pests and diseases and isolation from markets. Malnutrition, high maternal and child mortality, illiteracy, overgrazing and poor infrastructure are rampant in the area. The other sites are located in Uganda, Rwanda, Tanzania, Malawi, and Senegal. There are two projects located in Mali, and two sites in Nigeria.

Most of these communities suffer from similar maladies such as poor infrastructure, drought, isolation, no access to medical care, starvation and malnutrition, diseases, and lack of clean water and sanitation. The rugged terrain and isolated conditions make it difficult to travel or to communicate, and most of these people are living on less than $1 U.S. dollar per day. The experience highlighted from the Millennium Villages suggests that with political support, effective partnerships, and modest financial resources well within the bounds promised to Africa by the donor countries (though not yet delivered), villages across rural Africa can achieve the MDGs and escape the poverty trap.

# EPILOGUE

## What can we do?

I was in class, teaching a room full of college students about the social problems of children in Sub-Saharan Africa. A student that had remained quiet almost the entire course raised her hand. I acknowledge her, pleased that she wanted to take part in the discussion. She didn't have a question, but she did have a comment. Her comment was, "this class is depressing."

At first, I was a little defensive, but inwardly, I struggled with the question as much as she did. What can we do about this problem in Africa? I began to look at all the programs that I thought might be good for the region, and of course, the Millennium Village I visited in Bonsaaso was also very revealing. I came away with a good feeling about their work. But what about other programs, other agencies that were supposed to be working in Africa? What were they doing? Here are a few programs to examine for this purpose.

## USAID

*The United States Agency for International Development* is the United States federal government agency primarily responsible for administering civilian foreign aid. President John F. Kennedy created USAID in 1961 by executive order to implement development assistance programs in the areas authorized by the Congress in the Foreign Assistance Act of 1961.

According to its own website, foreign assistance has always had the twofold purpose of furthering America's foreign policy interests in expanding democracy and free markets while improving the lives of the citizens of the developing world. USAID has been the principal U.S. agency to extend assistance to countries recovering from disaster, trying to escape poverty, and engaging in democratic reforms.

In their own publications, the agency states that it works primarily in five major regions: Sub-Saharan Africa, Asia, Latin America and the Caribbean, as well as the Middle East. It also points out that they work in conjunction with other agencies. With headquarters in Washington, D.C., USAID claims to work with private organizations, universities, businesses, and other private and Non-governmental agencies. So, like the World

Bank and the IMF, USAID essentially is geared toward helping others, such as developing countries that are embroiled in poverty and other social issues.

USAID plans its work around individual country development programs tailored to the recipient countries. USAID missions reside in over fifty developing countries, consulting with each country's government and non-governmental organizations to determine which of their programs will receive USAID's assistance. As part of this process, USAID missions conduct socioeconomic analysis, design projects, award contracts and grants, administer projects (including evaluation and reporting), and manage flows of funds.

USAID missions are led by Mission Directors and are staffed both by USAID Foreign Service Officers and by development professionals from the country itself, with the host-country professionals forming a majority of the staff. The length of a foreign-service "tour" in most countries is four years, to give U.S. staff the opportunity to develop in-depth knowledge about the country. (Shorter tours of one or two years are permitted in countries of exceptional hardship or danger).

## Poverty Relief

Assistance projects in each country are authorized by the Mission Director under the direction of the U.S. Ambassador, USAID and State Department headquarters, and the Congress. The resident USAID mission administers and evaluates the assistance. After 1945, many newly independent countries needed assistance to relieve the chronic deprivation afflicting their low-income populations. Since its founding in 1961, USAID has continuously provided poverty relief in many forms, including assistance to public health and education services targeted at the poorest. USAID has also helped manage agricultural commodity assistance provided by the U.S. Department of Agriculture. In addition, USAID provides funding to NGOs to supplement private donations in relieving chronic poverty. But has USAID made a difference?

## Criticisms of USAID

One of the harshest critics of the USAID organization is Jeffrey Sachs, the person responsible for the Millennium Village Project, and director of the Earth Institute at Columbia University. Sachs has indicated his disapproval of USAID efforts on a regular basis, particularly in its avoidance of the HIV/AIDS and the malaria problem in Africa (Sachs, 2005).

He has also criticized the organization for its claim of its West African Water Initiative, which it says is on the "front line in the combat against water-related disease and death." So far, Sachs says, USAID has only contributed $4.4 Million over three years to this project. Sachs goes on to say that while West Africa has a population of some 250 million people, USAID is contributing less than a penny per day per person.

In another study it was learned that "in the case of the "Roll Back Malaria program," which USAID shaped and continues to influence, USAID's clout has actually harmed global health. Malaria rates have probably risen since 1998, when Roll Back Malaria was set up with the goal of halving rates by 2010. (American Enterprise Institute for Public Policy and Research, 2011).

This poor result is not for lack of resources; since RBM's inception, USAID has increased its malaria eradication budget from $18 million to $90 million (as of 2005). But the Agency's flawed malaria control strategy has rendered public and private investment unproductive.

The same study goes on to suggest that it is not clear exactly how these poor results have come to pass, again because USAID refuses to release details of the contracts, grants and cooperative agreements used to disburse malaria funds. But from the documentation that is available and communication with USAID staffers and contract employees willing to speak off the record to the same researchers, we know that USAID spends very little money purchasing the tools necessary to fight malaria effectively.

Others have criticized USAID for a number of different reasons. Some claim that the agency is acting more out of political notions than humanitarian. Some critics say that the US government gives aid to reward political and military partners rather than to advance genuine social or humanitarian causes abroad. Another complaint is that foreign aid is used as a political weapon for the U.S. to make other nations do things its way. Other critics have pointed out that the agency has worked in cooperation with the CIA and has overtly provided funds for opposition groups in other countries (Slavin, 2003).

While the criticism is not short in forthcoming, USAID has been improved by President Obama, who has attempted to raise the standards at the organization and to make it a priority in providing assistance to developing nations around the world. One of the most impressive uses of USAID has been its assistance for disaster relief. Recently, with the devastating earthquake in Haiti, USAID has been providing millions of dollars' worth of assistance. Clearly, there are some political ramifications for the agency, and some political issues with funding. Some members of Congress see no use for the organization these days, and are not apt to provide funding on a regular basis.

We have already seen that in certain parts of the world, natural disasters such as earthquakes, Tsunamis and floods can devastate communities and create a large population of street children and orphans. Funds provided for assistance during these emergencies can help alleviate those problems when they occur.

## The World Bank and the International Monetary Fund

The World Bank is a source of financial and technical assistance to developing countries around the world. Their mission is to help governments in developing countries reduce poverty by providing them with money and technical expertise they need for a wide range of projects—such as education, health, infrastructure, communications, government reforms, and for many other purposes.

The World Bank is one of five institutions created at the Bretton Woods Conference in 1944. The International Monetary Fund, a related institution, is the second. Delegates from many countries attended the Bretton Woods Conference. The most powerful countries in attendance were the United States and United Kingdom, which dominated negotiations.

For the poorest developing countries in the world, the bank's assistance plans are based on poverty reduction strategies; by combining a cross-section of local groups with an extensive analysis of the country's financial and economic situation the World Bank develops a strategy pertaining uniquely to the country in question. The government then identifies the country's priorities and targets for the reduction of poverty, and the World Bank aligns its aid efforts correspondingly.

## Criticisms

The World Bank has long been criticized by non-governmental organizations, such as the indigenous rights group Survival International, and academics, including its former Chief Economist Joseph Stiglitz, who is equally critical of the International Monetary Fund, the US Treasury Department, US and other developed country trade negotiators.

Noam Chomsky, (1999), criticizes the World Bank in its dealings with Haiti over the years. In fact, according to Chomsky, the World Bank-

USAID development strategy was initiated in 1981, which suggested the usual formula of "expansion of private enterprises," and minimization of "social objectives," thus increasing inequality and poverty. Chomsky reiterates that along with their suggestions, they told Haiti to reduce inequality and poverty and improve health and educational levels. Chomsky says:

> "In the Haitian case, the consequences were the usual ones: profits for U.S. manufacturers and the Haitian super rich, and a decline of 56 percent in Haitian wages through the 1980's—in short, an "economic miracle.""

In the 1980's, the most dramatic change in the World Bank occurred during the administrations of Ronald Reagan and Margaret Thatcher, who were adamant about developing countries adopting free market ideology. At that time, the World Bank and the IMF were the new "missionary institutions" that were going to change the world (Stiglitz, 2003). Most of their policies were being pushed onto poor countries that badly needed loans and grants.

## The International Monetary Fund

The IMF was also conceived at a United Nations conference convened in Bretton Woods, New Hampshire, United States, in July 1944. The 44 governments represented at that conference sought to build a framework for economic cooperation that would avoid a repetition of the vicious circle of competitive devaluations that had contributed to the Great Depression of the 1930s.

## The IMF's responsibilities

The IMF's primary purpose is to ensure the stability of the international monetary system—the system of exchange rates and international payments that enables countries (and their citizens) to transact with one other. This system is essential for promoting sustainable economic growth, increasing living standards, and reducing poverty.

In the 1980's, the two agencies (World Bank and IMF) became forever intertwined in their policies and their mission. The World Bank went beyond just lending money for projects like roads and dams, but began to provide support in the way of *Structural Adjustment Loans*. We have already seen that these programs are further exasperating the efforts of developing countries to improve. The World Bank offered support to developing countries after the IMF approved, and in turn, placed conditions on the countries which were detrimental to their development (Stiglitz, 2003). Other scholars have also been critical of the two agencies. Jeffrey Sachs called the policies of the World Bank and the IMF a "simpleminded view of poverty," (Sachs, 2005).

# UNICEF

*United Nations Children's Fund* was created by the United Nations General Assembly on December 11, 1946, to provide emergency food and healthcare to children in countries that had been devastated by World War II (UNICEF, 2011).

In 1953, UNICEF became a permanent part of the United Nations System. Headquartered in New York City, UNICEF provides long-term humanitarian and developmental assistance to children and mothers in developing countries. It also provides vital statistics and reports on children in developed nations.

UNICEF works in over 150 countries, and is a global humanitarian relief organization providing children with health care and immunizations, clean water, nutrition and food, security, education, emergency relief and more. Throughout this book, facts and figures about orphans, street children, and children living in poverty have been largely provided through the assistance of this organization.

UNICEF is part of The United Nations, which works for world peace. The main purpose of UNICEF is to make sure that children around the entire world get the care and education they need to grow up to be happy and healthy adults. UNICEF believes that children require special kinds of care and affection. If children don't receive good care, it can harm them forever. It is the only UN agency that is completely devoted to children.

UNICEF treats all children equally. It doesn't matter what religion, nationality, race, or gender a child is. UNICEF talks to different countries' government leaders and asks them to support the children in their country and to value their rights. UNICEF believes that there must be hope for a country's children in order for there to be hope for that country in the future. UNICEF helped design a special treaty called the Convention on the Rights of the Child. This lists the basic human rights of children. In 1989, it was formally accepted by the General Assembly of the UN. The Convention includes children's rights to:

- health care
- education
- a fair standard of living

- leisure and play
- protection from being exploited and abuse
- express their opinions

UNICEF works on projects that help children in over 150 countries around the world. Most of these projects help to keep children alive and healthy. One main goal of UNICEF is to continue to help children in countries that have dealt with wars and natural disasters. However, today UNICEF is dealing more with poverty and illnesses in the poorest countries of the world.    UNICEF studies which countries in the world have the most children dying at young ages. These countries are the places that are in urgent need of good health care for their children. UNICEF programs help countries drill new wells for clean drinking water. Some UNCIEF programs teach people about good hygiene and how to take care of the water supply in their communities.

UNICEF programs also teach mothers in poor countries to read, so they can take care of their children's health care needs by reading posters in health clinics, on medicine bottles and in books. UNICEF programs also help mothers improve their education so they can get a job to help their families.

UNICEF also has some programs to help give vitamins and vaccinations to children in poor countries to help them stay healthy. UNICEF also helps to break the cycle of poverty by helping to provide a good education. UNICEF talks to some nations' leaders to create laws that would make it illegal to have children work. UNICEF also has programs to help children who are homeless. They have reading classes, health check-ups, and sport activities for kids who are homeless. UNICEF works to make sure children get the love and support they need from their families, schools, and neighborhoods.

## Micro Lending and the Grammeen Bank

One of the most impressive tools for economic development for third world countries are *microloans,* which were initially created by the Grammeen Bank in 1976.    The founder of the Grammeen Bank is Muhammad Yunus, professor of Economics at Chittagong University in Bangladesh.

When I think back on the question by the student that announced that my class was depressing, I think of another question, and that is: *what can one person do?*    The more I thought about this question, the more I realized that one person, Muhammad Yunus, has changed a lot of people's lives through his efforts.

*Microcredit* is the extension of very small loans (microloans) to those in poverty designed to spur entrepreneurship. Generally, these individuals lack collateral, steady employment and a verifiable credit history and therefore cannot meet even the most minimal qualifications to gain access to traditional credit. The Grammeen Bank has reversed the conventional banking practices by removing the need for collateral (Yunus, 1999).

The Grammen Bank has created a system based on mutual trust, accountability, and cooperation. The system is based on the voluntary formation of small groups of five people to provide mutual, morally binding group guarantees instead of collateral. At first, only two people in the small group are allowed to apply for a loan. Depending on their performance on repayment, the other members are encouraged to apply. The repayment rate proved to be extremely successful at over 98 percent.

The success of the program has been astounding, and has helped families out of poverty all over the world. As of 2011, there were over 8 million borrowers, of which 97 percent were women. This fact alone is extremely significant, for when women are employed in providing income for their families, there is an immediate economic impact which is obvious. However, by keeping women in employment, the fertility rates go down, which helps some poor countries sustain economic development. It also empowers women, which is one of the goals of the Millennium Development Goals.

With 2,565 branches, GB provides services in 81,379 villages, covering more than 97 percent of the total villages in Bangladesh. Grameen Bank's positive impact on its poor and formerly poor borrowers has been documented in many independent studies carried out by external agencies including the World Bank, the International Food Research Policy Institute (IFPRI) and the Bangladesh Institute of Development Studies (BIDS). In 2006, The Grammeen Bank, as well as Muhammad Yunus.

Clearly, microcredit is one proven method of helping children and families out of the poverty trap. Programs that are adapted to the economic well-being of families will in effect reduce the chances of children growing up in poverty, and thus increase their chances of staying in families and off the streets. It would also increase the likelihood of children attending school rather than working to support their families, thus would likely reduce the street children population around the third world.

I firmly believe that microloans would work well in Sub-Saharan Africa. Clearly, many people have been helped out of poverty through this method. I could envision millions in Africa working in small, organized groups, creating small businesses that would assist them in accumulating income to support their families.

## Non-Governmental Organizations (NGO's)

Non-Governmental Organizations, or NGO's, as they are more commonly referred to, are organizations that are usually non-profit in origin, and are set up to assist in many different social arenas. The term originated from the United Nations, and although, some NGO's are not private entities, as they receive funding from State and National funding sources. However, most of the NGO's are working in areas in which social services are needed to provide assistance in eradicating poverty, health issues, and other such activities (OECD, 1988).

The number of internationally operating NGOs is estimated at 40,000, although each country has their own large number of these agencies. I worked for one such NGO in Peru, known as the Bruce Peru Organization. The organization, described in earlier chapters, provides free education for those children living in slums, shanty towns, and other poor areas, who cannot afford to go to school. Their purpose is to improve the education in third world countries. They supply these services in Peru, Bolivia, and other places, as well.

Many NGO's receive their funding from private donations, and many of the workers there are volunteers who travel overseas from the United States, Canada, and other developed nations. These volunteers work in service areas such as schools, orphanages, day care centers, family planning clinics, and many other such areas. NGOs have emerged in large part to bridge the gap between what governments and corporations can do and what society needs or expects. Since these first organizations came into prominence, many more NGOs have been established. Some are small organizations with only a handful of staff and volunteers. Others operate on a global scale. Whatever the case, NGOs continue to play a critical role in addressing needs of children and others on a grand scale. Clearly, in some areas, NGO's are offering services where no major programs are in place. NGO's may work in the most desolate of locations, and in the far reaches of Africa and beyond. Staffed by caring people and volunteers from all over the world, NGO's are making a difference worldwide.

In the case of Africa, while I was there working as a volunteer in the orphanages, it was evident that the volunteers were not only needed, but were largely doing most of the work. While qualified staff is sparse in some quarters, they are often neglectful and abusive, whereas volunteers are more caring and provide more of a nurturing environment than the staff in some of those facilities.

## Multinational Corporations

Some multinational corporations are also involved in helping the poor around the world. Some of them have made terrific strides in the reduction of children's social problems around the world. For example, The Microsoft chairman, Bill Gates, whose $27 billion *Bill and Melinda Gates Foundation* has made huge strides in providing funds to different areas of the world.

The foundation is led by CEO Jeff Raikes and Co-chair William H. Gates Sr., under the direction of Bill and Melinda Gates and Warren Buffett, and has a myriad of International as well as domestic programs to help the poor. For example, *Save the Children's Saving Newborn Lives* program, works in partnership with 18 countries to reduce neonatal mortality and improve newborn health. The *World Food Programme* is one branch of the foundation that seeks to bring food to 90 million people in 73 different countries.

Clearly, other multinational corporations could make a difference if they were to engage in activities as Bill Gates has done. If other large corporations step up to the plate, they could also make a difference in people's lives around the world, especially in Africa.

## A Final Word

I remember writing in my journal at the end of my research in Sub-Saharan Africa as I spent my last days there:

> I will miss Africa. In the midst of all this poverty and pollution, there's something mystical about it. For one thing, it's amazingly beautiful here. The trees, the rain forest, the jungles, the flowers, the friendliness of the people, and the way the breeze blows across the land. Then, of course, it's the children—not just the kids in the orphanages, or the street children, but children everywhere are special here. They seem happy just to be alive, and the next bowl of rice is just as good as the last one, and they will eat the next one with the same relish and desire. Everywhere I went, I was met by children, with their arms held out wide, their eyes glistening, with smiles pasted on their sweaty faces.

Oddly enough, one of the things I loved the most about Africa was the trees. The Baobab trees were spectacular, and appeared to be carved by the very hand of God himself. The rain is something that I found interesting about Africa. It was gentle rain, a type that the Navajo people in the American Southwest would call "female rain." However, it would leave villages full of mud because of the lack of paved streets. All the paths and dirt roads were quagmires, and large puddles of water would stand for days.

I loved hearing the local dialects of Akan, spoken by the people there. In my mind, I can still hear the melodious sounds of the Twi and Ga languages of the people of Ghana. The smells will always be with me, as well, from the burning trash to the open sewers in Accra, the Capital city. I can still remember the smell of yams being prepared for dinner, and Foo-Foo as it slid down my throat. I remember the Roosters crowing, and the Goats bleating outside my window every morning.

## Leaving Ghana

The day I left Ghana, the rain had started two days ago, and the Bush Road was a mess. Only a few brave Tro-Tro drivers were braving the mire of the slow, muddy roads. I took off walking toward the highway with my friend, Hugh, bags in hand, following the sides of the road, avoiding the major ruts and puddles, when a taxi driver pulled up and picked us up. My excitement was short-lived, as the taxi proceeded to get stuck in the mud. It took all three of us to push the cab out of the mud pit. Finally, we were on our way to the airport.

When I began this trip, I was hoping that I would be as fortunate as I had been in Peru about meeting good people and making friends with the other workers. The time I spent in Ghana exceeded that. I arrived at the airport, said goodbye to my friend, Hugh and settled in to wait for my plane. I already missed my friends in Africa, but I missed home more. In doing this type of research, there is a point that I call "satiation," where you have reached the critical conclusion of your work—not necessarily because you are through, but because you have had enough of it all. You are tired, the malaria medication is wearing on you, the nights are long and lonely, the days are longer and hotter, and you have seen poverty reeking out of every crack and corner.

Ethnographic research sometimes calls for a strong stomach as well as a strong mind. Watching children that are hurting everyday takes something out of you. Sometimes, it is unreasonable to expect yourself to be able to handle it all. The demands are relentless, and just as you want to sit inside out of the rain, you may need to go out and see how the street children are faring, and how they are surviving the elements. My arrival in Ghana was mystical if not magical. I had always dreamed of going to Africa. Even as a child, I had boyhood dreams of being there. I blame it on watching early "Tarzan" movies as a child with my cousin, and I was fascinated by the animals, the beauty of the jungle, and the mystique of the continent. Did Africa measure up to my dreams?

If I am going to compare the realities of Africa to those of my childhood impressions, I would say that it did not come close. I think everyone sees Africa as a place where wild animals abound and they envision caravans and Safaris and similar scenes. While those things do exist in Africa, they are not the general realities of the Continent. Indeed, I have only seen a small portion of a vast continent, and there are many more orphanages across Sub-Saharan Africa, some good, and some not so good. I can't see them all; therefore, my research is limited to the few that I can arrange while I am there. I can only see so many street children, conduct so many interviews, and while time is somewhat limited, I have to work fast with the time that I have. I also want to see the sights, and I managed to take in as much as I could.

I have seen the jungles, the Savannahs, the Rain Forests, the green mountains. I have experienced the rain, and the mosquitoes and the frogs and the giant toads that sound like gigantic monsters in the middle of a lonely night. I have gotten to know the Ghanaian people. They are people with great spirits, and a longing for something better. I have seen a country that once served as a model for independence across Africa, beginning with Kwame Nkrumah, the first president of Ghana. I have seen a country whose hopes were dashed with a coup that sent their great leader into exile, perhaps a plot by the American CIA, once again plunging the country into darkness.

I have seen a country that is struggling with extreme poverty, with hope lying fertile as the Millennium Villages continue to operate in Bonsaaso. It serves as a starting point in alleviating rural poverty in Ghana, as well as malaria in over 30 villages. This organization brings together the communities, the government, and other agencies as they address the problems of health care, education, sanitation, safe water, and the poor infrastructure of the region. I have also seen the big cities— crowded, vibrant, yet polluted with open sewers and improper waste management, lack of sanitation, toilets, or running water.

I have seen inside the country's many orphanages, and seen the dirty faces of children left homeless by the plagues of disease and death, the ravages of HIV/AIDS, drug addictions, child abuse, and abandonment. I have seen the distended abdomens of children who have been living on a diet that lacks the proper nutrients and proteins, as they suffer from malnutrition. I have seen children die of malaria, as they lay in bed with no medical treatment.

I have heard stories from my colleagues, working in government-run facilities, who tell of the Aunties (staff) who take donated items home with them, denying the children those same items. I saw firsthand, and heard stories of the staff laying down and going to sleep, leaving the orphans unsupervised, or leaving their care to a handful of foreign volunteers that have devoted their time in the orphanages.

I have heard stories of orphans being beaten at night when volunteers are not around. I have never seen the orphans eat anything other than rice, except for the occasional treats bought or brought by volunteers.

Life in Ghana is tough. They have very little, and they struggle daily to get by—those in rural areas have even less, and unless their problems are addressed—many of them will die of malnutrition, malaria, AIDS, diarrhea, typhoid, cholera, and other such diseases due to lack of medical care, lack of medications, shortages of doctors and nurses, and lack of proper sanitation, and safe water.

The infrastructure of the entire country is disastrous, as there are only a few paved roads. Most of the paved roads lead to the other major centers and regions, but beyond that, roads are generally dirt.

I will miss the rapport of so many wonderful people—intellectuals, adventurers, lovers of life, givers, takers, readers, talkers, tellers of tales, and drinkers. They will be missed. What I will not miss is the smell of poverty, pollution, burning trash, and the harsh conditions in which we lived daily.

As I am writing in my journal, we are flying over the last of Senegal, and are now in the middle of the Atlantic Ocean—possibly the same route taken by slave ships, carrying their cargo of captives across the sea to their ultimate destiny as slaves in a foreign land. They were taken from their families and their country, stripped of all their dignities, their culture, their identity, and their self-image. I will always remember the castles of Elmina and Cape Coast, as they are grim reminders of the Atlantic Slave Trade. I have seen the dungeons, the cells, and the dark tunnels where captured Africans were once taken and held in chains until they walked through those "doors of no return," and be carried off to the Americas as slaves. As I fly above it, I feel like I flew above most of the problems in Africa while I was there. It is one thing to go there, work, research, and see the problems. It's another matter entirely to live there permanently, and to endure the ravages of poverty and disease in which these people encounter on a daily basis. Soon, I would be home to my comfortable bed, my own home, my car, and my life.

Yes, Africa is still a mystical place. There are secrets there that may never be uncovered. Life is thought to have begun in Africa. Ancient man may go back millions of years to the dark forests of Africa, and the rest of the world may have even been populated first from African Hunters and Gatherers, migrating from the African continent to Asia and parts of Europe.

There are forests, and jungles, and animals, and mountains, and raging rivers, and malaria- carrying mosquitoes, and AIDS, and cholera, and war, and pestilence. There are children being forced into the military, to participate in conflicts, wars and rebellions. There are children being kidnapped and forced into brothels to become child prostitutes in the International Sex Tourism business.

AIDS is also taking its toll on the continent. It is destroying families, creating orphans who may have to live a life in an institution that will not properly provide for their development and care. Street children take to the streets rather than schools, while other children scramble to find work in mines and quarries, or in the military. All of these factors may be holding the continent back from developing.

It is fairly obvious that there is plenty of poverty and sadness, but there is also hope, and love, and happiness, and respect and honor. I believe that the people of Ghana will rise and become the bright star that will shine through Africa once again. It will take some time, but I believe that Kwame Nkruma's dream will once again shine.

# REFERENCES

American Enterprise Institute for Public Policy and Research, 2011.

Amnesty International, *Hidden Scandal, Secret Shame: Torture and Ill-Treatment of Children*, 2005.

Ardayfio-Shandorf, (1997). Changing Family Life in Ghana. Ghana University Press.

Beah, Ishmael (2008). *A Long Way Gone: Memoirs of a Boy Soldier.* Farrar, Straus and Giroux; 1st edition. New York.

Beauchemin, E. (1999). "The Exodus: The Growing Migration of Children from Ghana's Rural Areas to the Urban Centers." Catholic Action for Street Children.

Berlyne, D.E. (1960). Conflict, Arousal, and Curiosity. New York. McGraw Hill.

Bicego, G., Rutstein, S., & Johnson, K. *Dimensions of the emerging orphan crisis in sub-Saharan Africa,* in "Social Science and Medicine," Volume 56, Pp. 1235-1247.

Bolton, Giles (2008). *Africa Doesn't Matter: How the West Has Failed the Poorest Continent and What We Can Do About It.* Arcade Publishing. New York.

Briere, John (1992). *Child Abuse Trauma: Theory and Treatment of the Lasting Effects.* Newbury Park. Sage Publications.

Briggs, Phillip (2007). *Ghana.* Bradt Travel Guides. 4th Edition. UK.

Bowlby, John (1956). *Attachment.* Basic Books. New York.

Casa Alianza Study, Mexico City. 2010.

Child Soldiers Global Report, "Coalition to Stop the Use of Child Soldiers," 2008.

Chen J. A., Hicks W. W., Johnson S. R., Rodriquez R.C. (1990) "Economic Development, Contraception and Fertility Decline in Mexico." *Journal of Development Studies* 26 (17) 408-424.

Chomsky, Noam (1999). *Profit Over People.* Seven Stories Press. New York.

Colgan, Ann Louise, & Booker, Salih, "All Africa Archive." *Africa: Hazardous to Health: the World Bank and the IMF in Africa.* http://allafrica.com/stories/200204260615.html.

Cluver L, Gardner F. "Risk and protective factors for psychological well-being of children orphaned by AIDS in Cape Town: A qualitative study of children and caregivers perspectives." *AIDS Care*. 2007; 19(3):318–325

Davis, Mike (2006). *Planet of Slums*. Verso. London.

Denov, M. (2010), *Child Soldiers: Sierra Leone's Revolutionary United Front*. Cambridge: Cambridge University Press.

—. (2005) Child Soldiers in Sierra Leone, "Report prepared for the Government of Canada through the Canadian International Development Agency."

Drugs and Human Performance Fact Sheets. National Highway Traffic Safety Association. http://www.nhtsa.gov/people/injury/research/job185drugs/toluene.htm

Erikson, Erik (1994). *Identity and the Life Cycle*. W.W. Norton and Co. New York.

F. Porter, L. Blick, & S. Sgroi, "Treatment of the Sexually Abused Child," in S. Sgroi, ed. *Handbook of Clinical Intervention in Child Sexual Abuse*. Lexington Books. Lexington, Ma.

Family Housing Fund Report, "Homelessness and its Effects on Children," By Ellen Hart-Shegos Hart-Shegos and Associates, Inc. Editor: Anne Ray. December, 1999.

Fisher, R. (1998). *West African Religious Traditions: Focus on the Akan of Ghana*. Orbis Books. Maryknoll, New York.

Forrester Research, Inc. 2002.

Fraley C, Shaver PR. "Loss and bereavement: Attachment theory and recent controversies concerning "grief work" and the nature of detachment." In: Cassidy J, Shaver JR, editors. *Handbook of attachment theory and research*. New York: Guilford; 1999. pp. 735–759.

Frank, R. & Cook, Phillip (1996). *The Winner-Take-All Society: Why the Few at the Top Get So Much More Than the Rest of Us*. Penguin Books. New York.

Friedman, Thomas L. (2000). *The Lexus and the Olive Tree*. Anchor Books. New York.

Friedman, Thomas (2005*). The World is Flat: A Brief History of the Twenty-First Century*. Farrar, Straus, and Giroux. New York.

Ghazvinian, John (2008). *Untapped: The Scramble for Africa's Oil*. Harvest Books. Orlando, Florida.

Goffman, Erving. 1985. Behavior in Public Places: Notes on the social organizations of gatherings. New York. Free Press.

Guest, Emma (2001). *Children of AIDS: Africa's Orphan Crisis*. Pluto Press. London. UK.

Hanwanna, A. (2005). *Child Soldiers in Africa (The Ethnography of Political Violence)*. University of Pennsylvania Press; annotated edition. Philadelphia.

Hardoy, J., & Satterthwaite, D. (1989). *Squatter Citizen*. Earthscan Publications, Ltd. London.

Herr, Harvey, & Karl, Guenter, "Estimating Global Slum Dwellers- Monitoring the Millennium Development Goal 7, Target 11, for UN- HABITAT. 2001."

Hollingsworth, Jerry (2008). *Children of the Sun: An Ethnographic Study of the Street Children in Latin America*. Cambridge Scholars Press. Newcastle. UK.

Human Rights Watch, *The Scars of Death: Children Abducted by the Lord's Resistance Armies in Uganda,* Human Rights Watch Report, 1997.

Human Rights Watch, "A Briefing for the 4th UN Security Council Open Debate on Children and Armed Conflict," Child Soldier Use, 2003.

Human Rights Watch "Children's Rights." 2001. http://www.hrw.org/children/abandoned.htm. 4 Dec. 2001.

Hunter, Mic (1990). *The Sexually Abused Male: Volume 1: Prevalence, Impact, and Treatment.* Lexington Books. New York.

International Labor Organization, "Accelerating action against child labour." Report of the Director-General, International Labour Conference, 99th session, 2010.

International Labor Organization, "Combating the Trafficking of Children for Labour Exploitation in West and Central Africa (Phase II): Benin Country Annex" (ILO-IPEC 2000).

—. "Training manual to fight trafficking in children for labour, sexual and other forms of exploitation," *International Labour Office, International Programme on the Elimination of Child Labour* (IPEC). - Geneva: ILO, 2009 - 4 v.

—. (ILO). 2006. *Global child labour trends 2000-2004.* Geneva: ILO.

James, B. & Nasjleti, M. (1983). *Treating sexually abused children and their families.* Palo Alto, CA : Consulting Psychologists Press.

Kendal, Diane (2010). *Sociology in Our Times.* Wadsworth Publishing. Belmont, California.

Keilland, A., & Tovo, M. (2003*). Children at Work: Child Labor Practices in Africa.* Lynne Rienner Publishers Inc. Boulder, Colorado.

Kopoka, Peter A., "The Problem of Street Children in Africa: An Ignored Tragedy," *International Conference on Street Children and Street Children's Health in East Africa.* A working Paper. 2000.

Lurie, Mark, et al. "The Impact of Migration on HIV-1 Transmission in South Africa." *Sexually Transmitted Diseases*, Vol. 30, No. 2 (2003).

Mam, Somaly, (2008). *The Road of Lost Innocence: As a girl she was sold into sexual slavery, but now she rescues others. The true story of a Cambodian heroine.* Spiegel and Grau. New York.

Mills, C. Wright (1956). *The Sociological Imagination.* Oxford University Press. London.

NACADA, "Youth in Peril: Alcohol and Drug Abuse in Kenyan Children, 2004."

Naim, Moises, (2006). *Illicit: How Smugglers, Traffickers, and Copycats are Hijacking the Global Economy.* Anchor Books. New York.

Nolan, Stephanie (2007). *28 Stories of AIDS in Africa.* Walker and Company, New York.

Oberai, A.S. (1993). *Population Growth, Employment and Poverty in Third World and Mega-Cities.* Palgrove Publishing. Maryland.

Opiyo, P.A. et al, 2008, 'HIV/AIDS and home-based health care', International Journal for Equity in Health 7:8).

O'Kane, Claire. (2003) "Street and Working Children's Participation in Programming for their Rights." *Children, Youth, and Environments.* Vol 13(1).

OECD, Organization for Economic Cooperation and Development "Voluntary Aid for Development: The Role of NGOs", *OECD*: Paris, 1988

Parten, Mildred. "Social Play among preschool children." Journal of Abnormal and Social Psychology, 27, 243-269.

Piaget, Jean. 1962. *Play, dreams, and imitation in childhood.* New York. Norton.

"Privatization in Africa." 1998. Oliver C. Campbell White and Anita Bhatia. Directions in Development series, World Bank, Washington, D.C

Reader, John (1997). *Africa: A Biography of the Continent.* Alfred Knopf. New York.

Rediker, Marcus (2007). *The Slave Ship: A Human History.* Viking. New York.

Sachs, Jeffrey (2006). *The End of Poverty: Economic Possibilities for Our Time.* Penguin. New York.

Soma Wadhwa, "For sale childhood," *Outlook*, 1998.

St. Clair, William (2007). *The Door of No Return: The History of Cape Coast Castle and the Atlantic Slave Trade.* Bluebridge Publishing. UK.

Stillwaggon, Eileen (1998). *Stunted Lives, Stagnant Economies: Poverty, Disease, and Underdevelopment*. Rutgers University Press. New York.

Stiglitz, Joseph (1993) *Economics*. New York: W.W. Norton & Co.

*The Crusading Guide* Ghanaweb, 2005 http://www.ghanaweb.com/CrusadingGuide/article.php?ID=4172

The Factbook on Global Sexual Exploitation, Donna M. Hughes, Laura Joy Sporcic, Nadine Z. Mendelsohn, Vanessa Chirgwin, Coalition Against Trafficking in Women, 1999.

Takyi & Oheneba-Sakye, (1994). *African Families at the Turn of the 21st Century*. Kendal Hunt Publishing Company. Dubuque, Iowa.

The Ghana Living Standard Survey, taken from the Ghana Human Development Report (2007).

Thomas L. Friedman Reporting: *The Other Side of Outsourcing*, 2005. DVD. Discovery Communications Inc.

The Earth Institute, Columbia University. Lead Partners. 2011. http://millenniumvillages.org/

UN HABITAT, "the Challenge of Slums: Global Report on Human Settlements," London 2003.

United Nations Population Division. 2009. World Population Prospects: The 2008 Revision. New York.

United Nations Human Development Report, 2010.

United Nations, "Human Development Reports," United Nations Development Program, 2011. http://hdr.undp.org/en/statistics/

—. "The report of the Secretary-General on Children and Armed Conflict in Sudan," 2009.

—. End Poverty 2015, Millennium Development Goals. *UN Web Services Section, Dept. of Public Information.* United Nations. 2010 http://www.un.org/millenniumgoals

UNAIDS, UNICEF, USAID. 2004. Children on the Brink 2004: *a Joint Report of New Orphan Estimates and a Framework for Action. Washington, D.C.*

UNICEF, (2006), *State of the World's Children, Excluded and Invisible*, Pp. 40-41.

—. *State of the World's Children report*, (2009).

—. "Progress for Children Report," December 2007.

—. "The Issue of Child Domestic Labor and Trafficking in West and Central Africa," as cited in "The Worst Forms of Child Labor: Country-Wise Data, October 2000.

—. "Background: Protecting Children from Trafficking" (www.unicefusa.org/ct/background_2.html); cited October 30, 2001.

—. Children and Armed Conflict - International Standards for Action (The Human Security Network, UN Special Representative of the Secretary General for Children and Armed Conflict, 2003)

—. "The Machel Study," 1996.

—. "Progress for children: Achieving the MDGs with equity," September, 2010.

—. "Africa's Orphaned Generations," New York, November, 2003.

—. United Nations Development Programme, "toward Universal Primary Education: investments, incentives, and institutions." 2010.

UNESCO, Global Monitoring Report, "Education for all: the Quality Imperative," 2005.

—. Global Monitoring Report, 1998.

—. 2011 Global Monitoring Report, "The hidden crisis: Armed conflict and education."

—. *Association for the Development of Education in Africa,* 2001.

University College London Development Planning Unit and UN-HABITAT, *Understanding Slums: Case Studies for the Global Report on Human Settlements* 2003.

U.N. Human Development Report (1999).

U.S. Department of State, June 1, 2011. Bureau of African Affairs: Ghana. http://www.state.gov/r/pa/ei/bgn/2860.htm

U.S. State Dept., Trafficking in Persons Report, 2007.

USAID, From the American People, Official Website. http://www.usaid.gov/index.html

Van de Walle & Meechers, (1994). *Overcoming Stagnation in Aid Dependent Countries: Politics, Policies, and Incentives for Poor Countries.* Cambridge University Press.

Wessells, Michael (2006). *Child Soldiers: From Violence to Protection.* Harvard University Press. Cambridge, Ma.

White, C., & Bhatia, A. (1998). *Privatization in Africa.* World Bank. Washington, D.C.

Wolack, J., Finkelhor, D., & Mitchel, K., 2005. "Child Pornography Possessors Arrested in Internet-Related Cases." National Juvenile Online Victimization Study. National Center for Missing and Exploited Children.

World Bank, *Global Economic Prospects and the Developing Countries, 2000,* p. 29.

World Health Organization, World Malaria Report, 2010.

WHO/UNAIDS, Report on the HIV/AIDS Epidemic, 1998.

World Health Organization, "A Profile of Street Children," Mental Health Determinants and Populations, Department of Mental Health and Substance Dependence, Geneva, Switzerland.

WHO, "World Malaria Report, 2010."

World Bank, *Global Economic Prospects and the Developing Countries, 2000*, p. 29.

World Food Programme, 2011. Official Website: http://www.wfp.org/

Yunus, Muhammad, (1999). Banker to the Poor: Micro-lending and the battle against world poverty. Public Affairs books. New York.

Zastrow, Charles (2000*). Social Problems: Issues and Solutions.* Wadsworth, Inc. Kentucy.

# INDEX